THE METTERNICH CONTROVERSY

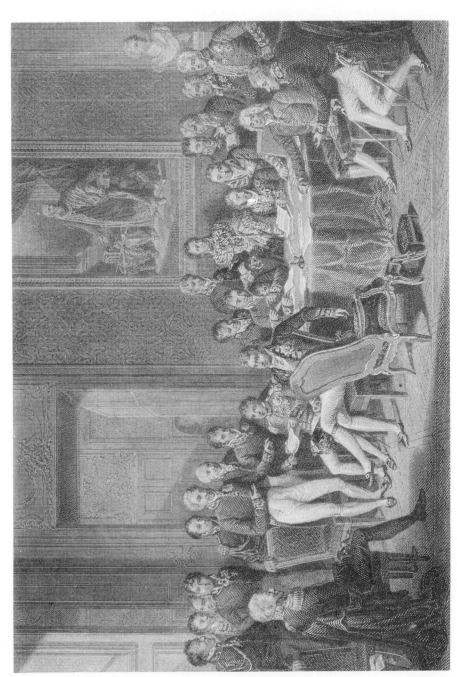

The Congress of Vienna, 1815. Metternich is in left foreground, standing. Line engraving after J. B. Isabey. *(The Granger Collection)*

THE
METTERNICH
CONTROVERSY

Edited by **ENNO E. KRAEHE**
University of Virginia

HOLT, RINEHART AND WINSTON
New York • Chicago • San Francisco • Atlanta
Dallas • Montreal • Toronto • London • Sydney

Cover illustration: Metternich in 1859. Photograph taken shortly before his death. *(The Granger Collection)*

Library of Congress Catalog Card Number: 74–135125
SBN: 03–078100–0
Printed in the United States of America
1 2 3 4   008   9 8 7 6 5 4 3 2 1

CONTENTS

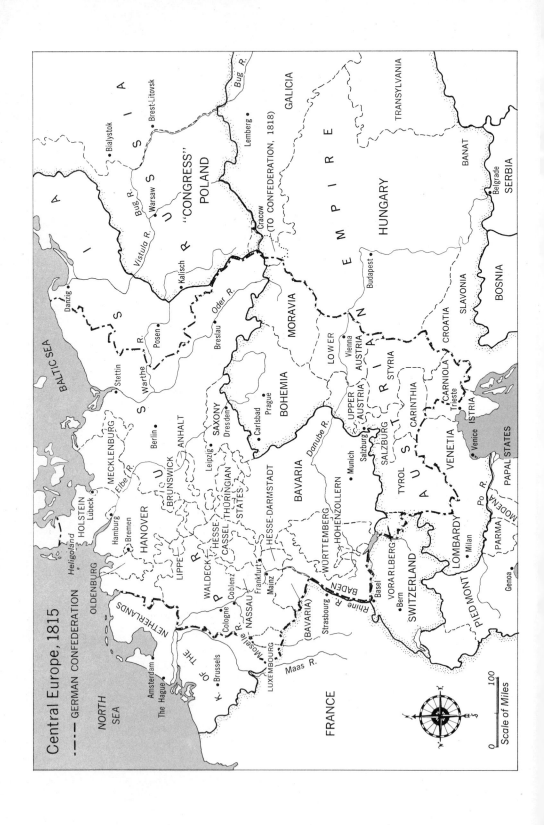

Central Europe, 1815

— · — GERMAN CONFEDERATION

NORTH SEA

BALTIC SEA

NETHERLANDS

OF THE

The Hague •

Amsterdam •

Brussels •

LUXEMBOURG

Maas R.

Moselle R.

Cologne •

NASSAU

Coblenz •

Frankfurt •

Mainz •

LIPPE

WALDECK

HESSE

CASSEL

HANOVER

Bremen •

Hamburg •

HOLSTEIN

Lübeck •

Heligoland

OLDENBURG

MECKLENBURG

Elbe R.

Berlin •

ANHALT

BRUNSWICK

Leipzig •

THÜRINGIAN STATES

HESSE-DARMSTADT

BADEN

(BAVARIA)

Strasbourg •

Rhine R.

WÜRTTEMBERG

HOHENZOLLERN

BAVARIA

Munich •

Danube R.

Carlsbad •

Prague •

BOHEMIA

SAXONY

Dresden •

Breslau •

Oder R.

Posen •

Warthe R.

Stettin •

Danzig •

P R U S S I A

S I L E S I A

Vistula R.

Bug R.

Kalisch •

Warsaw •

"CONGRESS" POLAND

Bialystok •

Brest-Litovsk •

R U S S I A

Lemberg •

Cracow •

(TO CONFEDERATION, 1818)

GALICIA

TRANSYLVANIA

Budapest •

HUNGARY

E M P I R E

LOWER AUSTRIA

Vienna •

MORAVIA

UPPER AUSTRIA

Salzburg •

SALZBURG

STYRIA

CARINTHIA

A U S T R I A N

TYROL

VORARLBERG

SWITZERLAND

Basel •

Bern •

Strasbourg

FRANCE

PIEDMONT

Genoa •

Milan •

LOMBARDY

Po R.

VENETIA

Trieste •

CARNIOLA

ISTRIA

Venice •

PAPAL STATES

MODENA

PARMA

CROATIA

SLAVONIA

BANAT

Belgrade •

SERBIA

BOSNIA

Scale of Miles

0   100

INTRODUCTION

When Clemens Lothar Wenzel von Metternich-Winneburg-Beilstein officially assumed the duties of Austrian foreign minister in October 1809, no one
could have foreseen that in a few years the Era of Napoleon would be succeeded
by the Age of Metternich. A disastrous war had just been terminated and a peace
signed which pressed the Austrian Empire to the verge of dissolution. Napoleon
was master of Europe and Austria an independent power in name only. Yet five
years later Metternich was widely hailed as the "prime minister" of a coalition
that defeated Napoleon and at the Congress of Vienna in 1814–1815 redrew the
boundaries of Europe. From then until his dismissal in 1848 his influence was
such that he was sometimes called the coachman of Europe—truly a reversal of
fortune since the dark days of 1809, when he had advised his emperor that "we
can seek our security only in adapting ourselves to the triumphant French
system."

That Metternich should give his name to a third of a century of European
history is all the more remarkable when one considers that he was neither a general, nor a crowned head, nor a native Austrian, nor a man of relentless drive, iron
will, or conspicuously original ideas. He was a professional diplomat and a count
of the Holy Roman Empire, from the German Rhineland; he had a reputation for
indolence and deviousness, and a tendency to bore people with vain boasts and
pendantic clichés. Who, after all, likes to hear even his best friend remark,
"Twenty times a day I have to say to myself, dear God, how often I am right and
the others wrong"? And who would not wince at the platitude that "of all things,
nothing is so fatal as error"? Add to these Metternich's reputation for chasing—
and catching—women (a serious two-volume study bears the title *Metternich and
the Women*[1]), and the picture one could easily get is that of a shallow, frivolous
nature, certainly not the stuff of which greatness is made.

During his lifetime and for several generations afterward evidence such as
this was readily, even gleefully, used by his political opponents to discredit him.
Even when in the 1880s European archives began to open their holdings for the
Metternich period and an eight-volume edition of his private papers appeared,
historical judgment remained generally hostile. Metternich had fought a life-

---

[1] This and all other works referred to in this introduction are fully cited in Suggested Additional
Reading, p. 133.

long campaign against the great movements of liberalism, democracy, and nationalism. He had defended the monarchical principle against republicanism and had opposed the unification of Italy and Germany. It is not surprising that historians writing in the heyday of liberalism, in the era of the Third French Republic, Bismarck's German Empire, and Cavour's Kingdom of Italy (which included much former Austrian territory), should see in Metternich an unadorned reactionary and foe of human freedom, a completely negative obstructionist, who failed to comprehend the vital forces of his time.

This remained the conventional picture of Metternich until after World War I. Metternich had once said that "in a hundred years the historian will judge me quite differently than do all those who pass judgment on me today." And so it was. Nationalism, an important cause of the war and the destruction of the Habsburg monarchy, no longer looked so glamorous or constructive. In the world of the Bolshevik revolution, liberalism no longer seemed the answer to all problems. In Germany even Bismarck's work was questioned as possibly too narrowly based. The man who had stood for peace based on an equitable balance of power and social stability through observing "principles" now seemed, if not more virtuous, at least more comprehensible. Thus a young Swiss scholar Werner Näf saw in Metternich the architect of European federalism and in his system a precursor of the League of Nations. The most comprehensive rehabilitation of Metternich's reputation, however, was accomplished by an Austrian, Heinrich Ritter von Srbik. His massive biography, published in 1925, pictures Metternich as a serious, coherent thinker who rose far above Austria's particular problems and became a great statesman in the tradition of what we often call the good European. Srbik's views, which are represented by two selections in this volume, never attained as wide acceptance as the earlier, nineteenth-century interpretation, but it is safe to say—to put it the way Metternich himself might have—that Srbik provided against the abnormal force in one direction a necessary countervailing force in the opposite direction. The resulting clash of ideas has inspired most of the research and writing on Metternich ever since, as the reader of this anthology will observe.

Clemens Metternich was born on May 15, 1773, in Coblenz, at the confluence of the Rhine and Moselle rivers in the German Rhineland. The area was Roman Catholic in religion and strongly influenced by French culture; politically it belonged to the Holy Roman Empire—or simply the "Reich," as it often appears in the literature. Metternich's father, Franz Georg, was an imperial count, which meant that he held his estates of Winneburg and Beilstein directly from the emperor. Theoretically, therefore, he was almost an independent prince, the equal of such great princes as the duke of Württemberg, the elector of Bavaria, or even the king of Prussia. In actual political and military power, however, he and several hundred other members of the high German nobility like him were insignificant. They therefore sought their security in rallying around the em-

peror, whereas the mightier princes tended to resist imperial directives that came
from far-off Vienna.

Franz Georg Metternich accordingly took employment in the imperial service, and it was with a similar future in mind that Clemens studied law with
Christophe Guillaume Koch at the University of Strasbourg and Nicholas Vogt
at the University of Mainz. These details are important because some historians
trace Metternich's later concepts of natural balances in the social and political
order largely to the teaching of these men. Other historians (perhaps skeptical
of professors' influence on students) assign more importance to what happened
next: the conquest of the Rhineland by revolutionary France, the seizure of the
Metternich properties, and the flight of the family itself to Vienna. However
one explains Metternich's implacable opposition to revolution and his later
programs of repression, there can be no doubt that this direct, personal involve-
ment early in his career made a deep and lasting impression.

Indeed, on their arrival in Vienna in 1794, father and son took it for granted
that Emperor Francis II and his government shared their concern about losing
imperial territory and would fight to destroy the revolution. Only gradually
did they come to realize that the Holy Roman Empire (Reich) was but one of
several concerns of the House of Habsburg, the others being the interests of its
own dynastic lands, some of which (notably Hungary) lay outside the Empire.
The distinction between a German-imperial point of view and a Habsburg, or
Austrian, point of view was vividly demonstrated by the treaty of Campo Formio
in 1797. In this treaty Emperor Francis recognized all French conquests west of
the Rhine, exchanging his own so-called Austrian Netherlands, which was part
of the Empire, for Venice, which was not. This was a small loss for him, a great
loss for the Empire. As for the Metternichs, they were eventually compensated
for their losses by the abbey of Ochsenhausen in southern Germany.

Clemens Metternich meanwhile was gradually initiated into the Austrian
point of view. First he broke into the tightly drawn ranks of the Austrian aristocracy, marrying Eleonore von Kaunitz, granddaughter of the great Austrian
chancellor.[2] Then he entered the Habsburg diplomatic service, beginning in
1801 with a post in Dresden, advancing in 1803 to Berlin as minister and in 1806
to Paris as ambassador. These years saw a major defeat for Austria (Austerlitz
in 1805) and, forced by Napoleon, the complete triumph of the Austrian over the
imperial point of view. In 1804 an Austrian empire was proclaimed, and for the
first time the Habsburg lands were bound together in a single state. Two years
later the Holy Roman Empire was dissolved and replaced by a league of states
known as the Confederation of the Rhine, or Rheinbund. In the process of
liquidating the old empire the lands of hundreds of families like the Metternichs,
as well as many imperial cities and ecclesiastical estates, were absorbed by the

---

[2] Wenzel Anton von Kaunitz (1711–1794).

larger states. Ochsenhausen, for example, was taken into the new kingdom of Württemberg. The princes who were awarded these territories naturally tended to favor Napoleon and dreaded the possibility that his reorganization of Germany might someday be undone.

After 1806 this undoing was precisely the aim of many dispossessed German aristocrats who shared the fate of the Metternichs. One of these was Count Johann Philipp von Stadion, who became Austrian foreign minister in 1806 and hoped that through reforms in Austria and patriotic appeals in Germany he could incite the masses to rebel against the Napoleonic order. The result was the ill-fated war of 1809, mentioned earlier, which Austria fought single-handedly and lost. If space had permitted, the present volume could have included an interesting section on Metternich's role in bringing about this war. The traditional view, based on Metternich's inflammatory reports from Paris and the assumption that a dispossessed imperial count would naturally desire revenge, holds that Metternich aided and abetted Stadion's war policy at every turn. This interpretation has recently been challenged, however, by a German scholar, Manfred Botzenhart, who on the basis of new archival material contends that Metternich actually counseled peace. If Botzenhart is correct, Metternich had already abandoned a somewhat emotional "German-imperial" outlook in favor of a more calculated strictly "Austrian" one earlier than was previously believed. Indeed, Botzenhart goes further than this, holding that Metternich's stand was not merely Austrian but European, disclosing at this early date that sense of broad, statesmanlike responsibility which his defenders admire most. Botzenhart's conclusions are still very debatable but they are useful here because they help define a persistent problem in interpreting Metternich: Was he in the main an ideological crusader against revolutionary change, a narrow Austrian diplomat, or a statesman of European outlook?

The question of Metternich's relationship with Napoleonic France looms even larger for the period after the war. As foreign minister from 1809 he considered Austria too weak to do anything but ingratiate itself with the victorious Bonaparte; he carried out this policy by "tacking, evading, flattering" as he put it, his master stroke being the marriage of Francis's daughter Marie Louise to the French emperor. In 1812, as a Franco-Russian war approached, he allied Austria with France, certain that he was backing the winner. This of course was not the case. Contrary to all expectations Tsar Alexander crushed Napoleon's Grand Army; by early 1813 he was pursuing its remnants into Germany, and had compelled Prussia to switch over to the Allies, which included, besides Russia, Great Britain and Sweden. In the treaty of Kalisch (February 28) Prussia was promised much territory for this action. Despite enormous pressure to follow Prussia's example, Metternich embarked instead on a tortuous diplomatic manuever of armed mediation between the opposing sides. His particular proposals varied according to circumstances, but essentially they aimed at restoration of a balance of power based on confining France to the Rhine and Russia to the Vistula, and making Germany a neutral zone in between. After protracted negotiations and the signing of an armistice on June 4, 1813, the Allies accepted Metternich's terms in the treaty of Reichenbach on June 27. With Bonaparte, Metternich's nego-tiations reached a climax at two dramatic conferences, a personal confrontation in Dresden on June 26 and a peace congress in Prague in early August. Napoleon refused Metternich's terms; on August 12 Austria declared war.

Such is the background for the first set of readings assembled here. For understandable reasons many French historians including such masters as Albert Sorel and Edouard Driault, over the years have insisted that Metternich never really desired a negotiated peace but deceived Napoleon in order to gain time — time to rearm, time to persuade Emperor Francis to betray his son-in-law, time to convince a war-weary Europe that Napoleon alone obstructed peace. Metternich himself claimed in later years that this was so and liked to picture himself as the conqueror of Napoleon. This interpretation is perhaps the most common view, though not always so acidly set forth as in the selection by Louis Madelin. Notice, for example, his scorn for the "European" point of view. Others take the opposite position, arguing that Metternich was sincere in his peace efforts and, if anything, partial to Napoleon. The evidence for this conclusion depends to a large extent on a detailed analysis of the negotiations beginning with the armistice of June 4. That is why the excerpts from the work of Enno E. Kraehe and that of Hellmuth Rössler demand close attention, patience, and the use of a map. Although Rössler and Kraehe agree about Metternich's *intentions*, they disagree about the *wisdom* of his policy. Considering the options open to the foreign minister, Kraehe believes he chose correctly, even brilliantly. Rössler, on the other hand, endorses the criticism made by Stadion, who in 1813 as an envoy favored the same kind of all-out war against France that he had conducted in 1809 as foreign minister. Stadion's program, moreover, was hostile to Napoleon's German satellites, whereas Metternich preferred to appease them. In evaluating these disagree-ments the reader should ask if Stadion's background as a dispossessed imperial count influenced his views, and if so, why was the same not true of Metternich? What was Russia's role? How did Metternich and Stadion differ in their assess-ments of Tsar Alexander's intentions?

For better or worse, Metternich's peace program was in general realized at the Congress of Vienna (1814–1815), where Clemens, at age forty-one and now elevated from count to prince, played a leading role (some would say *the* leading role, while others would assign this honor to Lord Castlereagh of England). In the ensuing years the new European order was consolidated at other international conferences: at Aix-la-Chapelle in 1818, Carlsbad in 1819, Vienna and Troppau in 1820, Laibach in 1821, and Verona in 1822. These were the years of Metter-nich's greatest influence, the years when his course was set in most respects for the remainder of his career. Metternich himself denied the existence of a system, but he talked so incessantly about his principles that people fell naturally into the habit of referring to the "Metternich system."

In any case, the debate in the second section of this book revolves to a considerable extent around the status of Metternich's principles. Srbik, as previously suggested, was the first to regard them as statements of genuine intellectual commitments and guides to action. In the excerpt presented here he outlines what he considers to be the intellectual content of Metternich's ideas and argues that the excellence and appeal of these ideas account for Metternich's ability to hold office and retain his influence so long. Despite its cumbersome style, this is a famous essay in the literature on Metternich. Karl Groos, in his pioneering psychological study, is not concerned so much with the substance of Metternich's principles as with the fact that he was so obsessed with them. Only a vain, almost paranoiac personality would act the way he did, Groos concludes. Henry A. Kissinger sees Metternich's principles not so much as consisting of political theory but rather as reflecting the profound insights of an experienced statesman into the limits and possibilities inherent in his particular position. He agrees with Srbik, however, that the key to Metternich's success was the widespread acceptance of his ideas. Paul W. Schroeder concentrates more on Metternich's deeds than on his words and insists that the two were often contradictory as well as shortsighted and superficial. His criticism of the Srbik school is direct and explicit.

In analyzing these sharply conflicting views, the reader should ask, first, if the evidence used is as contradictory as the conclusions. Do the writers draw on different kinds of sources or do their differences arise from different interests? Remember that a psychologist and a political scientist may start with different preconceptions and ask different questions. But Srbik and Schroeder, who disagree most, are both historians. Does Srbik really discuss Metternich's own ideas, or is he a name-dropper trying to associate his hero with prestigious philosophers? Does Schroeder consider realistically what alternatives Metternich had? Perhaps each of the writers has a part of the truth. Perhaps when all their qualifications are taken into account, their disagreement is less than it seems.

Probably the most important of Metternich's creations was the German Confederation, founded at the Congress of Vienna and further developed at the Carlsbad conference of 1819 and the Vienna conference of 1820. It was controversial from the beginning. Essentially, it represented an accommodation with Napoleon's former allies, the princes of the Confederation of the Rhine, and dashed the hopes of the old imperial nobility (including Metternich's father) for a restoration of the Holy Roman Empire. German nationalists were disappointed because they considered a loose confederation no worthy substitute for a genuine united German state. Liberals complained because the federal constitution contained only the barest hint at parliamentary government within each state and established for the Confederation as a whole only an assembly of diplomats called the federal diet. The Prussians, moreover, resented the privileged position Austria seemed to have as president of the Confederation. Finally, even the former wards of Napoleon, like the kings of Bavaria, Württemberg, and Saxony, and the grand duke of Baden, who should have been most satisfied with the Confederation, resisted every effort to give it effective powers. Some of them moreover, in order to mobilize public opinion behind them and encouraged by Alexander of Russia, introduced constitutions of their own.

Discontent manifested itself in various ways, only two of which need be mentioned here. One was a reform movement within the Prussian government to strengthen the state internally and in Germany by granting a constitution and a central representative body. The leaders were Wilhelm von Humboldt, Hermann von Boyen, and—some of the time—the chancellor, Prince Karl August von Hardenberg. The other conspicuous expression of discontent came from German youth. In the universities faculty and student activists issued manifestos, staged demonstrations, and organized a network of clubs called Burschenschaften. At a lower social level young men joined gymnastic societies (Turnvereine) organized by Friedrich Ludwig Jahn to promote physical fitness as a prerequisite to political reform. In 1817 a demonstration and book burning at the Wartburg, a castle near Jena, caused great anxiety among the governments. Two years later anxiety turned to panic when a student name Karl Ludwig Sand murdered a reactionary writer, August von Kotzebue. In the midst of widespread fear of revolution Metternich called the Carlsbad conference to agree on repressive measures, taking care in advance to obtain the cooperation of the king of Prussia. The notorious Carlsbad Decrees against revolution, against the universities, against the press, and against the sovereignty of individual states resulted.

With this background the reader should be able to follow the debate presented in the third section. The first excerpt is from a renowned work by Heinrich von Treitschke, who in his day was a passionate champion of German unity under Prussia. To him, Austria was an alien state and Metternich a scoundrel who cynically destroyed freedom and the wholesome development of Germany for Austria's own interest. Treitschke's vehement anti-Austrian bias, however, should not lead one to discount his scholarship completely; his is one of the few nineteenth-century diatribes against Metternich that still has value today. Like many others, Treitschke considers the threat of revolution something trumped up by Metternich in order to intimidate Prussia. Not so, says Srbik in the next excerpt; the threat of revolution was real and Metternich honestly believed it so—as did the Prussians, with whom he dealt honorably. Beyond that even this great admirer of Metternich has difficulty defending his hero, concluding that his action, though sincerely motivated, was wrong. The suppression of freedom is after all never easy to defend, regardless of provocation. The contribution of Peter Viereck, however, attempts such a defense—not by praising the police state but by discrediting its victims, many of whom, he claims, were not the decent and idealistic souls usually pictured. The reader may decide for himself if it is plausible to see precursors of Hitler's storm troops among the youth of a century earlier, but even so the question remains whether repression is ever justified. The last selection in this section, another contribution by Henry A. Kissinger, represents a partial return to Treitschke's position in that Kissinger sees the Carlsbad Decrees not so much as a matter of ideology but as a diplomatic maneuver to establish Austrian domination over Germany. Where Treitschke condemns, however, Kissinger admires. Yet even if Kissinger is correct, does this in any way affect the moral issue of suppressing freedom? Moral judgments aside, the four pieces in this section taken as a whole pose the further question: Did Metternich exploit the revolutionary scare in Germany to consolidate Austria's power, or did he use Austria's power to head off revolution?

After Metternich's triumph in Germany and a comparable one in the suppression of revolution in Italy in 1820–1821, his prestige was such that he was made state chancellor, a position that gave him a voice in the internal affairs of the Austrian Empire. Actually the new title made little difference, for Metternich had always been free with advice on all aspects of government, and the Emperor Francis, as an absolute monarch, could of course still do as he pleased. In any case, important questions arise regarding Metternich and Austrian internal affairs, the subject of the fourth section in this volume.

The Habsburg monarchy was a collection of provinces of widely different size, population, wealth, and ethnic makeup. One tradition (called Josephinism after Joseph II, the famous enlightened despot of the eighteenth century) held that only by centralizing administration and standardizing the law throughout the realm in a modern way could the monarchy be held together and effectively governed. The contrary argument was that only by catering to the customs and peculiarities of the various provinces could trouble be avoided. This position, in turn, was subdivided into a conservative outlook, which favored strengthening the traditional aristocratic diets of the historic provinces, and a more radical approach, which aimed at satisfying the claims of *nationalities,* regardless of provincial boundaries. This distinction did not matter so much in ethnically homogeneous provinces like Lombardy and Venetia (where the old guard had been destroyed by Napoleon in any case), but it was important in Bohemia, where the Germans had the upper hand over Czechs, and in Hungary, where the Magyars if allowed to follow their traditional constitution would rule Croats and several other nationalities.

Few writers have a good word to say for the policies of Francis, who leaned strongly toward Josephinism, or his son, Ferdinand (1835–1848), who was feebleminded. The question here is whether Metternich had any constructive ideas. If so, what did he do to put them through and what was his share of the blame for the stagnation? A. J. P. Taylor credits Metternich with perspicacity, but criticizes his remedies, particularly his hope of revitalizing the provincial diets, as inadequate and unrealistic. The reader may well ask how much Taylor is influenced by his belief that no solution was possible because nationalism and the Habsburg monarchy were irreconcilable. Arthur G. Haas challenges this view not only in extolling Metternich's plans for provincial reform but also in claiming that "national feeling" had not yet developed into the incorrigible nationalism of a later time. The great misfortune for Austria, says Haas, was the stubborn pursuit of centralism by Emperor Francis, who ignored Metternich's proposals. Did Metternich try hard enough to have his way? Should he have resigned when his policy was repudiated? Taylor obviously regards the matter as unimportant; and Haas contends that Metternich's resignation would have served no good purpose. Viktor Bibl, on the other hand, makes the issue central to his severe indictment, holding that Metternich's only concern was to stay in office despite the ultimately fatal consequences for Austria. He also blames Metternich for the failure to revitalize the provincial estates—a reform which Haas credits the chancellor with trying to achieve and which Taylor contends would have done no good. How persuasive is Bibl's evidence for Metternich's corruptibility? Can Metternich, or any man, be blamed for things that happen almost a century later? In the final piece in this group Robert A. Kann reverses Bibl's verdict, arguing that Metternich's very integrity prevented his embarking on reform plans that would have violated his principles. Metternich had reached a "tragic impasse." How different is this conclusion from Taylor's simple contention that nothing could be done? Is a statesman's first duty to his principles, as Kann implies, or is Bibl right in insisting that if a man sees a way out for his country, he should take it, regardless of his personal interest and feelings?

With the revolutions of 1848 we come to the end of Metternich's active career. He lived on until 1859 and continued to offer advice, but only in a private capacity. The question raised by his departure is that of his responsibility for the revolutions. Must not the "coachman of Europe" for a third of a century be blamed? Or was he only one of the horses? In a sense this issue is simply an extension of those considered in previous sections and needs no further explanation, but in all well-run debates summations are in order. Veit Valentin states the case against Metternich, and Hugo Hantsch defends him. Which of the other writers in this collection might be called as witnesses? On which side and on what particular points? Can one admire Metternich and still blame him for the revolutions of 1848?

Today, more than a century after his death, the controversy about Metternich is a lively as ever. In assembling the readings for this volume it was not necessary to dredge up contrived disputes or questions long since settled; only the excerpt from Treitschke dates from before World War I, but it has intrinsic interest and continuing relevance. Moreover, all the writers are serious, informed scholars, with more than an incidental interest in Metternich. Regrettably some of the most important have had to be omitted. Werner Näf, mentioned earlier, made major contributions both in his own writing and in that of his students at the University of Bern. Several Italian scholars would have been included if space had permitted. Bertier de Sauvigny in France, the leading authority on Metternich today, is missing only because his works, though numerous, do not lend themselves to excerpting. They are, however, strongly recommended. Without deprecating Metternich's abilities as a thinker, Bertier nevertheless finds the main sources of the chancellor's statesmanship in the concrete problems he faced.

Much research remains to be done. Some disputed points will be settled by the facts uncovered. Most, however, will remain disputed because historians differ in their philosophies, their methods, and their own historical experiences. Their task is to analyze the complex forces that bear on such people as Metternich, yet they themselves are shaped in the same way. The questions they ask are often generated by their own times. That is why Metternich is so much discussed today. No man ever had more experience than he in conducting diplomacy in a time of social change and revolution and in a world where the conventional rivalries of states are cut across by antagonisms of class and ideology. He lived, slept, and dined with such problems as domino effects, isolationism versus world order, when and where to intervene in other states' affairs, striking a balance between external strength and domestic needs.

His performance remains controversial, but lest the reader grow discouraged and adopt the vulgar maxim that "it's all a matter of opinion," he should ask two further questions. Does he know more about the Age of Metternich now than when he began? Does he know more about his own world? *Answers* may differ but *knowledge* advances. That at any rate is the faith of a scholar.

In the reprinted selections footnotes appearing in the original sources have in general been omitted unless they contribute to the argument or better understanding of the selection.

After Napoleon's sensational defeat in Russia in 1812, Metternich undertook to mediate between the belligerents. In midsummer 1813, the negotiations reached a climax in a meeting with Napoleon in Dresden, a peace conference in Prague, and Austria's entry into the war. Many historians, especially in France, have contended that Metternich was only playing for time and deceived Napoleon about his peace plans. The view is passionately argued by LOUIS MADELIN (1871–1956), renowned for his monumental sixteen-volume work on Napoleonic France. His opinion of Metternich, however, is more succinctly stated in an earlier work, which provides the material used here. The excerpt begins directly with the Dresden conference.*

Louis Madelin

Traitor to France

The interview took place on the 26th of June in the Marcolini Palace where Napoleon was installed. He received Metternich in a long gallery opening out of his own room. At first he was affable, but his expression soon clouded as he surveyed the inscrutable features of his visitor—that "plaster face," as the Tsar called it. "But for your disastrous intervention," he declared, "peace would by now have been made between the Allies and myself. . . . Confess it—ever since Austria assumed the role of mediator she has no longer been on my side; she is no longer impartial, she is against me." Metternich protested—peace depended entirely on the moderation of the Emperor of the French. "Very well then,

let us discuss terms. I consent. What do you want?" The Minister sought refuge in vague generalities and the Emperor grew impatient. "Let us be more explicit," he exclaimed. "I have offered you Illyria[1] as the price of your neutrality. Does that suit you? My army is quite strong enough to bring the Russians and the Prussians to reason, and all I ask of you is neutrality."—"But why should Your Majesty not double his forces?" Metternich had the effrontery to ask. "The whole of our army is yours for the asking!" The lie annoyed the Emperor, but he was anxious to convince Metternich that he could

[1] The Illyrian provinces were created by Napoleon out of territories on the Adriatic Sea ceded by Austria in 1809.—Ed.

*Reprinted by permission of William Heinemann, Ltd., and G. P. Putnam's Sons from *The Consulate and the Empire, 1809–1815* by Louis Madelin, translated by E. F. Buckley (2 vols.; London: William Heinemann, Ltd., 1923–1938), vol. II, pp. 219–226. Footnotes omitted.

win without the help of Austria, and he proceeded to launch forth on the strength of his armies. But damn it all, what did the Coalition want and what was Metternich doing in Dresden? Yes, he thought so, they wished to despoil him, and if he acceded to some of their demands, they would immediately insist on more. "In short, you want Italy, Russia wants Poland, Prussia Saxony, and England Holland and Belgium. You are all aiming at nothing less than the dismemberment of the French Empire!" Metternich must have admired his wonderful insight. "Yes," continued Napoleon, "I should have to evacuate Europe, half of which I still occupy, lead back my legions, arms reversed, across the Rhine, the Alps and the Pyrenees, and place myself and my future at the mercy of those whose conqueror I am to-day! What sort of a figure do they expect me to cut before the French people? Your Emperor is strangely mistaken if he imagines that a mutilated throne in France can afford refuge for his daughter and his grandson! Ah! Metternich, how much has England paid you for playing such a part against me?" It was a slip of the tongue prompted by rage, and, as it escaped his lips, the Emperor, thoroughly exasperated—or wishing to appear so—threw his hat on the floor. In 1811, in the Tuileries, Metternich would have picked it up; now he pretended not to have seen it. Napoleon, pacing up and down the gallery, continued to boast about his armies; he would crush all his enemies as he had done before! Now and again his foot touched the wretched hat, and at last he angrily picked it up.

Our authority for the whole of this interview consists of a note dictated by the Emperor to Maret[2] soon after it took place and two accounts given by Metternich himself. But it is impossible for the historian to be quite clear as to what may possibly have been arranged between the two parties. The only words of the interview that bear the undoubted stamp of truth are those with which it closed, for they confirm the fact that, in spite of all, Napoleon was . . . resolutely convinced that, when all was said and done, the Emperor of Austria, who was such a "good father," would find he had not the heart to compass the ruin of the King of Rome's[3] throne. Suddenly he resumed a cordial tone and placing his hand on Metternich's shoulder, said coaxingly: "Do you know what is going to happen? You are not going to make war on me!"

In his heart of hearts, Metternich had been more frightened than he confessed in his Memoirs, in which he naturally blew his own trumpet. As a matter of fact, he had not dared to submit a single definite proposal. He continued the interview with Maret. He was genuinely anxious. Was the Austrian army sufficiently prepared to secure the Allies the crushing and decisive victory they required? For Austria, defeat would mean annihilation. He enquired of Schwarzenberg[4] how soon he would be ready to join in the conflict and on receiving his reply played the part of the prince bountiful, offered to obtain an extension of the armistice till the date mentioned by the Marshal, and announced his departure for the 30th. But Napoleon wished to see him again; this time he showed him nothing but cordiality, and told him that if the armistice were prolonged he would send deputies

---

[2] Hugues Bernard Maret, Duke of Bassano, French foreign minister.—Ed.

[3] King of Rome was the title of Napoleon's son by Marie Louise, hence also grandson of Emperor Francis.—Ed.

[4] Prince Karl Philipp zu Schwarzenberg, Austrian general soon to be commander-in-chief of the Allied armies.—Ed.

to the Congress. Metternich took his departure; he had some difficulty in obtaining the consent of the Allies to a prolongation; and having done so it meant postponing the Congress until the 12th of July. Whereupon the Emperor left Dresden to inspect the Elbe line.

Just as he was getting into his carriage he was handed a despatch which made him turn pale; the news it contained was calculated to make his position in Europe even more difficult. The lamentable Spanish venture had ended in disaster! A series of mistakes of all kinds had enabled Wellington to return to the war-path and Joseph[5] had been obliged to leave Madrid. In spite of this he had insisted on at last exercising the authority of Commander-in-Chief that had been conferred upon him; but Wellington, who had forced the passage of the Douro, had assumed such a menacing attitude that the King, seized with panic, made a mad rush for the Pyrenees with his troops. Caught up at Vittoria and forced to fight on the 17th of June, he handed over the command to his Chief of Staff, Marshal Jourdan, who proceeded to make all the mistakes he should have avoided. His incapacity lost him the battle and he retreated in disorder to the foot of the Pyrenees. Spain was lost—and under the worst possible conditions. True, Suchet was still in possession of Catalonia and Joseph's army had not yet crossed the mountains. But this was all that remained of a once magnificent army destined sooner or later to be swept out of the country.

Napoleon had not the smallest doubt where the responsibility lay. He knew that it was Joseph who had made a hash of the whole business, and the first order

he sent was to deprive him of the command of the troops that had been driven to bay in the Pyrenees and hand it over to Soult, who would at least do his best to stop this "shameful" retreat. The King, completely disgraced, was relegated to the Château de Mortefontaine, where he had an estate, and forbidden to leave it or to receive anybody. Thus his unfortunate "Catholic Majesty," who three months previously had regarded himself as the successor of Charles V, was virtually placed under lock and key. As a matter of fact, the Emperor was determined he should not come to Paris and interfere with the conduct of the Regency.

* * *

The Congress was on the point of opening and the representatives of France had to attend it under the worst possible auspices. For Metternich still regarded it as a mere blind, an attitude shared by the Allies, as is proved by their choice of plenipotentiaries. It was only reasonable to expect that at a gathering convened for the ostensible purpose of deciding the fate of Europe, the Powers would have been represented by their leading Ministers, men like Nesselrode and Hardenberg.[6] But Prussia sent a subordinate named Humboldt, whose sole recommendation was his abysmal hatred of France, while Russia's emissary was an agent of the international crusade against Napoleon, a certain Baron Anstedt, who was also an Alsatian *émigré*. Furthermore these two men were not to conduct any negotiations; they were not, at any stage of the proceedings, to deal with the French representatives, but were merely to submit through Metternich the de-

---

[5] King of Spain, 1808–1813, oldest brother of Napoleon.—Ed.

[6] Count Karl Robert von Nesselrode, Russian foreign minister; Baron (later Prince) Karl August von Hardenberg, Prussian chancellor.—Ed.

mands to which Napoleon's plenipotentiaries were to reply through the same
medium. It will readily be understood
that the Emperor showed but little
inclination to countenance this impudent
farce.

He delayed sending his plenipotentiaries. He insisted, in the first place,
that Caulaincourt[7] should be summoned
to a "meeting" and not ordered to appear
before a "court." But this gave rise to a
general upheaval among all his followers
in Dresden—the Emperor, they declared,
was throwing away the last chance of
peace. Fouché, whom he had summoned
from Paris, for the sole purpose of
preventing him from intriguing there,
was intriguing in Dresden. But the most
dangerous adviser of all was Caulaincourt himself, who . . . ever since his
sojourn in St. Petersburg, had been a
"European"; in fact, he openly confessed
as much to Metternich, and, blinded
by his sincere belief in the enemy's good
faith, regarded the Emperor, his master,
as the only disturber of the peace. If, in
spite of this, the latter appointed him his
representative, it was, in the first place,
because he still regarded him as a faithful
friend, and, secondly and chiefly, because
he knew him to be *persona grata* in
Europe. However, he hedged him round
with the strictest and most precise instructions, insisting that from the out-
set all excessive demands should be met
by the claim of *uti possidetis*[8]—unless,
of course, mutual concessions could be
agreed upon.

Caulaincourt always remained convinced that had he been left a free hand

he would have persuaded the Allies to
retreat. It was a curious illusion; for at
that very moment Metternich was losing
no opportunity of telling certain confidants that he had ceased to trouble his
head about this or that condition—war
was imperative! Meanwhile, in response
to an appeal from the Allied Sovereigns,
Bernadotte[9] had gone to Trachenberg
to reach an understanding with them on
the subject of the coming operations.
He was to command the northern army
and with 130,000 men was to descend
from Pomerania direct on Saxony, while
Blücher, at the head of an army of
120,000 men, raised in Silesia, was to
attack straight ahead in the direction of
Dresden and Schwarzenberg, with 120,000
Austro-Russians, was to debouch from
Bohemia and take the French armies on
the flank. The Congress had become a
mere formality conducted to please Metternich and to serve his Machiavellian
purpose.

On arriving at Prague on the 28th of
July, the Duke of Vicenza, though convinced that he would find grave reasons
for anxiety, was simple-minded enough
to imagine that his grace and charm
would suffice to remove them. However,
he overrated the power of his personality.
Some historians baldly assert that he
turned traitor. I have endeavoured to
elucidate this distressing problem and
have been unable to come to the conclusion that Caulaincourt was guilty of actual
treachery. But, if any faith is to be placed
in the testimony of the enemy's plenipotentiaries, there is certainly room for all
manner of suspicions. Apparently he led
Metternich to believe that by making
heavy demands on Napoleon he would

[7] Armand Augustin Louis, Marquis de Caulaincourt, Duke of Vicenza, French diplomat in Napoleon's entourage; earlier ambassador to Russia, in
1814 foreign minister.—Ed.

[8] Meaning that the bargaining would begin on the
basis of the territory each side then held.—Ed.

[9] Jean Baptiste Jules Bernadotte, former marshall
of Napoleon, after 1810 Prince Royal of Sweden,
and since 1812 ally of Russia.—Ed.

be serving the cause of France. "Send us back to France either by means of peace or by means of war, and thirty million Frenchmen and all the enlightened servants and friends of the Emperor will call down blessings on your head." This assertion is so preposterous as to be almost incredible. "I am just as much of a European as you can possibly be," he is also said to have declared—and this, at any rate, sounds less improbable. It has always been a pose among a certain class of Frenchmen to pass themselves off on occasion before foreigners as being more European than French.

But the other "Europeans," who still remained natives of their respective countries, quickly exploited this imprudent candour. There was no need for Metternich to deceive Caulaincourt; the latter deceived himself. All he had to do was to confirm him in his error, and he swore that Austria had not the ghost of an agreement with any other Power. Caulaincourt, thus reassured, felt confident of coming to terms. But whom was he to come to terms with? He did not even see the foreign plenipotentiaries, who, shut up in their own rooms, conducted negotiations entirely by means of notes sent through the Austrian Chancellor.

Meanwhile the Emperor, who had nothing whatever to do with this sorry farce, had set out for Mayence, where he was to meet the Empress. As a matter of fact, he wished to be nearer Paris in order to gauge the state of public opinion in France.

What must chiefly have alarmed him was the depression of his Ministers and those high functionaries who, as Molé[10] confessed, "in their official pronounce-ments professed deep devotion to their chief and confidence in the present and the future, which they one and all proceeded to deny in the bosoms of their families, where they did nothing but abuse him, making the domestic hearth re-echo with the curses they called down upon his head." In order to combat this secret pessimism, which to-day is aptly termed defeatism, the Emperor, in the presence of the Empress Regent and those who had come with her from Paris, behaved as though he were overflowing with optimism and good cheer. As a matter of fact, he was to a certain extent sincere, for he felt that a great victory would set everything right, and was convinced that it lay within his grasp. Moreover, he had received a letter from Murat[11] which gave him great pleasure—the Gascon was leaving Naples to take up his command again. "To love and serve you is a necessity for him," Caroline had written to her brother, and Joachim himself, in placing his sword at the disposal of his Emperor, was making honourable amends for past delinquencies. "Never doubt my heart, Sire; it is better than my head!"

Napoleon returned to Dresden well satisfied. By the 4th of August he was once more installed there and filled his General Staff with astonishment by his gaiety and good spirits. And yet he knew that before long he would have to meet an enemy whose strength had been doubled by the arrival of Bernadotte in Germany and the adhesion of Austria to the Coalition. As a matter of fact, Maret was writing to tell Caulaincourt that it was precisely because the Emperor found himself in a difficult position, but one

---

[10] Louis Mathieu, Count Molé, Napoleonic official. — Ed.

[11] Joachim Murat, king of Naples and husband of Napoleon's sister Caroline. — Ed.

that was worthy of his genius, that he was filled with secret joy.

Meanwhile he was still endeavouring to restrain Austria, and on the 5th of August wrote from Dresden to Caulaincourt telling him to get into personal touch with Metternich. But the latter managed to avoid a private conversation, and on the 7th of August made up his mind to inform Caulaincourt of the conditions demanded by the Allies. "Austria," he added, "is not yet allied with Russia and Prussia," we know how much truth there was in this!—"But she will join the cause of Europe if peace is not made by the 10th!" Thus the Emperor was given only forty-eight hours in which to answer Yes! or No! to what amounted to an ultimatum. And even if he accepted this ultimatum the signature of peace was by no means certain. For these conditions, declared Metternich, were "apparently" attached by the Allies to any "arrangements" which might "lead" to a general peace.

Caulaincourt, the "good European," showed no indignation but urged his master to lose no time. As the Allied plenipotentiaries were showing signs of anxiety at this juncture (what if Napoleon were to accept!), Metternich informed Humboldt that "on the 11th war would certainly be declared, whatever Napoleon replied!"

Caulaincourt's report did not reach Dresden until the morning of the 9th. An answer was to be received by midnight on the 10th. Napoleon read the Note which, though it demanded from him three-quarters of his possessions outside France, contained no definite assurance that if he made these sacrifices he would secure the neutrality of Austria. He had always declared that he would never tolerate having an answer wrested from him with a dagger at his throat, and it was not until the morning of the 10th that he despatched a Note in which he accepted some of the proposals and rejected others. As it did not reach Prague on the 10th, at midnight Metternich declared the Congress dissolved. But how could a Congress be "dissolved" which, owing to the way in which matters had been conducted, had never really "met"? Be this as it may, on the morning of the 11th of August, 1813, Austria declared war. But, according to Metternich, Austria would in any case have joined the conflict on that date. From beginning to end the Congress had been a mere farce; Nesselrode, who was behind the scenes all the time, confessed as much. "Never has there been so ludicrous a Congress," he wrote.

Nevertheless, this farce had secured the results expected by those responsible for it. "How strong Napoleon must feel to imagine he can refuse so advantageous a peace!" wrote Princess Radziwill with obvious sincerity. This Prussian aristocrat must have believed in the good faith of the Allies; the peoples of Europe also believed in it, but, what was far more dangerous, France, like Caulaincourt, believed in it too. And already from Prague the myth was spread abroad which within the space of four months was to be confirmed by the Declaration of Frankfort—Napoleon, in his mad pride, had "refused an advantageous peace!" He had criminally hurled two million souls back into the maelstrom of war! From the indignation to which such a belief was bound to give rise, even more than from the success of its arms, did the Coalition expect the triumph of its cause and the downfall of its enemy.

In direct opposition to Madelin, some other writers believe that Metternich's mediation maneuver was a sincere effort to reach an accommodation with Bonaparte. The point is illustrated with a selection from a work on Metternich by ENNO E. KRAEHE (b. 1921), which is used here because it encompasses as well the closely related question of how to deal with Napoleon's German allies. In France as in Germany, the argument runs, appeasement was the best of the available alternatives, in particular better than the unlimited war recommended by Count Johann Philipp Stadion, Metternich's predecessor as foreign minister. The excerpt begins with the armistice of Pläswitz signed on June 4 by Napoleon and the Allies.*

Enno E. Kraehe

Wise Appeaser of France

In order to progress from an armistice to a peace conference Metternich calculated that the allies must be convinced that their Kalisch[1] plans would be respected while France would be required to retire at least beyond the Rhine, surrendering the German territory she had annexed east of the Rhine, dissolving the Rheinbund,[2] and evacuating Italy. On the other side Napoleon would have to be convinced that he might retain influence in Germany and Italy while neither Russia nor Prussia nor Austria would be, from the French point of view, dangerously augmented. As the two conditions were contradictory, both sides would have to be somewhat misled, not necessarily by devising compacts that Metternich intended to violate, but by luring the rivals into a situation where, their expectations proving illusory, they might make mutual concessions under the threat of Austria's joining the other side if one or the other should refuse. This is the red thread running through the complex, often bewildering negotiations that led to Metternich's famous meeting with Napoleon at Dresden in

---

[1] Not literally but in effect the treaty of Kalisch (February 28, 1813) awarded Saxony to Prussia and the Duchy of Warsaw (the major part of Poland) to Russia. — Ed.

[2] German name of the Confederation of the Rhine. — Ed.

---

*From Enno E. Kraehe, *Metternich's German Policy*, Vol. 1: *The Contest with Napoleon, 1799–1814*. Copyright © 1963 by Princeton University Press. Pp. 173–186, 269–272. Original footnotes omitted. Reprinted by permission of Princeton University Press.

June. It was the last chance to solve the Rheinbund and Saxon-Polish problems at the same time and to Austrian advantage.

To impress the allies Metternich chose as the bearer of the Austrian program not the regular envoy, Lebzeltern, but Count Stadion, the one man who commanded confidence in St. Petersburg and who could be counted on to give Metternich's directions the strongest and most bellicose interpretation. It was also an advantage for Metternich to remove this firebrand from Vienna and the immediate vicinity of the emperor. Employing the hero of 1809 in this fashion had in fact been Metternich's plan since the first of the year, but Stadion, refusing association with a policy of appeasement, had steadfastly declined all assignments until Metternich should prove his determination to fight. The required proof was the mobilization of the army. Since that had now been ordered, Stadion eagerly accepted his appointment, the more so as he might now more effectively oppose a peace, which he no less than Metternich believed Napoleon might accept.

The instructions that Stadion carried to allied headquarters in early May contained the outline of what Metternich called a "good" peace. Except for demanding the return of Austria's former share of the Duchy of Warsaw and a vague reference to the restoration of Prussia to her former status in North Germany (points one and two), Metternich's program gave the impression that he desired nothing less than Russia and Prussia did—which in many respects was true. He proposed, in order: (3) the surrender of all territory annexed by France east of the Rhine; (4) the independence of Holland; (5) the surrender of all provinces annexed by France in Italy; (6)

the restoration of the pope; (7) the return to Austria of all territory taken from her after the peace of Lunéville; (8) "the cessation of Napoleon's supremacy in Germany"; and (9) the removal of Italy from French protection. This would be a *good* peace, Metternich suggested, one that he would be willing to strive for at a parley. He added, however, that to induce Napoleon to attend a conference more moderate terms would be necessary, for which reason agreement must be reached on a *minimal* program. The latter Metternich divided into two parts, Austria's own minimum terms and those minimum claims of the other powers which she recognized and would support. The Austrian minimum consisted of the recovery of Illyria,[3] a new frontier with Bavaria, and the dissolution of the Duchy of Warsaw. The other minimum included the return of South Prussia to Prussia, Napoleon's renunciation of all territory east of the Rhine, and his "renunciation of the Confederation of the Rhine at least in part or with modifications."

Never had Metternich chosen his words with such care. The dissolution of the Duchy of Warsaw implied, but did not absolutely necessitate, a repartition of the country so that Russia could not acquire the duchy intact—which was Austria's main concern. The reference to South Prussia suggested but did not explicitly state that Prussia's fair share of Poland was limited. Most ingenious, however, was the provision about the Rheinbund. The Kutusov declaration[4] had emphatically called for its dissolution, among other reasons, in order that Saxony could be dealt with differently

---

[3] The Illyrian provinces composed of provinces ceded by Austria to France in 1809.—Ed.

[4] On March 25 the Russian Commander, General Michael Kutusov, called on all Germans to turn on Napoleon.—Ed.

from the other states. But this is precisely what Metternich wanted to avoid; and in addition Napoleon was not likely voluntarily to surrender his German position as long as the war with England continued. Metternich hoped, apparently, that the allies, and possibly Stadion himself, would construe Napoleon's "renunciation of the Confederation of the Rhine" to mean its dissolution. Hence in Stadion's instructions he did not explain the somewhat different plan he intended to offer the French. At any rate, when Stadion met with Nesselrode and Hardenberg at Goerlitz on May 13, Nesselrode gained the impression that Austria would demand nothing less than the dissolution of the Rheinbund and the reconstruction of Prussia on a basis consistent with the treaty of Kalisch.

While Stadion was presenting Austria's case at Goerlitz, Count Bubna[5] arrived at Dresden with Metternich's proposals for Napoleon. Again the Austrian minister called for French surrender of her right-bank departments, the return of the Illyrian provinces and the dissolution of the Duchy of Warsaw. This time, however, he made it explicit that dissolution of the duchy meant repartition, "the use of its present domains for the reinforcement of the intermediate powers." Another change was that the frontier adjustment toward Bavaria which had been requested of the allies was shifted to an adjustment in Italy, presumably because, if the Rheinbund was not dissolved, Metternich would not violate his own principles by taking territory from it.

As for the Rheinbund itself, Metternich insisted that Austria did not wish to challenge Napoleon's protectorate for her

own ends but that the allies were bound to bring the matter up, and so he might as well state his position: namely, the conviction that "the independence of the German states under the guarantee of the great powers would offer, both to France and to the rest of Europe, real advantages for the chances of tranquility which such an order of things would establish. In admitting the incontestable principle that nothing would better assure the repose of the great empires than the interposition of another political body suited to diminish the natural friction between great masses, we pronounce the fate of Germany."

There it was—the intermediate plan. Napoleon would renounce his exclusive protectorate but retain influence in Germany through an *international* protectorate. The Rheinbund would remain intact, not as the instrument of any power but to secure the repose of all the powers. Prussia would abandon her designs on Saxony, and Austria would forego her slice of Bavaria. Here and there "modifications" could be made as mentioned in Stadion's instructions, but basically this was Metternich's solution of the German problem.

For the moment, however, neither camp was interested. On May 16 both Hardenberg and Nesselrode, who were now involved in negotiations with England, insisted that the independence of Italy, Holland, and Spain be added to the minimal program, and made it clear that the terms pertained only to a preliminary, not a definitive peace. They also rephrased Metternich's minimum to remove all doubt about "the dissolution of the Rheinbund, the independence of Germany, and the return of the annexed provinces in North Germany." On the other side Napoleon, whose military position appeared to be improving and who

---

[5] Count Ferdinand von Bubna, Austrian general and diplomat, after 1815, commander of Austrian forces in Italy—Ed.

in any case could hardly believe that allied and Austrian demands would remain fixed, once more rejected Austria's offer of mediation.

If Metternich's purpose had been merely to expose Bonaparte's intransigence, he could simply have published his terms. In fact, so far as the effect on Emperor Francis was concerned, the knowledge that Napoleon had refused even to attend a conference on such terms should have been more convincing than his rejection of the conditions at the conference itself. Since Metternich, however, genuinely desired both a peace conference and a peace without actually using Austria's armed forces, he continued his efforts. Under the sobering influence of the battle of Bautzen, he now went to the extremity of offering Napoleon a chance to approve in advance peace terms which Austria might then officially demand of him. Were such an accord reached, Metternich said, Austria would back it with her full military strength. Toward the allies, on the other hand, his attitude stiffened, and Stadion was able to induce Hardenberg and Nesselrode to accept a program milder than Austria's previously proposed minimum and considerably more compatible with what Bubna had first suggested to Napoleon.

The trick was turned by dividing the project into two parts, a *sine qua non,* which Austria was prepared to support with her army, and a set of terms for which she would plead but not fight. In the first group there remained of the previous minimum the award of Illyria to Austria and the dissolution of the Duchy of Warsaw. A third point mentioned the aggrandizement of Prussia "resulting from this dissolution"—an obvious effort to undermine the Kalisch pact although the phrase did not literally contradict the treaty. The fourth point concerned the trans-Rhine territory of France known as the 32nd military district. In all previous propositions the entire area was to have been unconditionally ceded by France. In the new formula this was true of only Hamburg and Lübeck, the remainder of the area being reserved as the subject for "a possible agreement" at a general peace conference. Thus the only immediate goal in this regard was to disrupt the continental system and satisfy Russia's demand for freedom of commerce in the Baltic.

Such were the terms *sine qua non.* The two points which Austria would support but not to the point of breaking up the conference were the clause about the Rheinbund, and the reconstruction of Prussia "as much as possible to her dimensions of 1805." But note: since the fate of the Rheinbund no longer represented an Austrian commitment, Metternich was now willing to adopt phrasing more congenial to the allies. Hence, for the first time he expressly mentioned not only the abolition of Napoleon's protectorate but also "the dissolution of this confederation." In this context, of course, the concession meant nothing. Should a peace conference materialize, he could easily offer as a compromise his plan for preserving but neutralizing the Rheinbund, and this maneuver continued to be the basis of his appeals to France.

There was one other problem. The allies at that very time were putting the final touches on a treaty of alliance with Great Britain, which was in fact signed on June 15 at Reichenbach. It provided for British subsidies and a guarantee of Prussia's 1805 extent. In return Britain was promised the restoration of Hanover and, above all, that no separate peace would be signed. Therefore even if Hardenberg and Nesselrode had not required it as a simple matter of precaution, their obligation to England now made it necessary to apply the terms of mediation to a *preliminary* rather than a final peace. This Metternich himself was willing to do, not only because the terms of the preliminary peace fell short of his major goal, the concomitant withdrawal of France and Russia from Central Europe, but also because England would now be implicated in any future peace conference. British participation had, to be sure, the disadvantage that England would probably insist on the liberation of Holland and Spain, but it would also give Metternich one more chance to establish an entente with the island empire and interpose a truly formidable force between Napoleon and Alexander. With Great Britain in attendance the conference would have been a veritable "Congress of Vienna" a year ahead of time, and with Napoleon's headquarters still in Dresden the Saxon-Polish question could hardly have taken the form it later did.

With several minor modifications the program concerted by Stadion, Hardenberg, and Nesselrode was finally endorsed by Alexander when Metternich personally interceded with him at Opotschna on June 19. It was formalized in the treaty of Reichenbach on June 27: if by July 20 Bonaparte had not accepted the four *sine qua non* points as the basis for a preliminary peace, Austria would join the allies, declare war, and accept the broader allied peace proposals of May 16 as "the program of the peace to be striven for in common." The last proviso was subject to various interpretations. . . .

Napoleon, meanwhile, impressed by, or at least curious about Metternich's visit to the tsar, extended an invitation for a similar interview at Dresden. Metternich has left two accounts of the meeting. One, written many years later and stressing the confrontation of two philosophies, the clash between the man of balance and the man of limitless ambition, exploited the poetical possibilities to the utmost. The other was a terse report composed at the time for the information of Francis, which corroborates, so far as it goes, a much fuller account given from the French side by Caulaincourt, with whom Napoleon discussed the meeting immediately afterwards. Essentially Metternich represented Austria as the loyal ally "ready to range herself at [Napoleon's] side with all her forces," if only he would listen to reason. Admitting the poor prospects of a general peace, he stressed the advantages of the continental terms Austria offered. Italy and Spain were not even to be subjects for discussion, he reminded the emperor, while the renunciation of the protectorate over Germany would cost him "a mere title, without depriving him of the natural influence that his position and his power would preserve for France."

On the surface Bonaparte was scornful, calling the sacrifices Metternich demanded worse than the effects of four lost battles, and too high a price to pay for the Austrian alliance. He took special delight in refusing to cede Illyria and maliciously intimated that the entire mediation maneuver was a bluff designed to extort the province from France. His real estimates, however, were different. Illyria, he told Caulaincourt, would only be the beginning. Austria "wants something else; she wants to reconquer her influence in Germany, then in Italy; she wants the protectorate of Germany." Metternich's repeated efforts, through Schwarzenberg and Bubna, had been in vain after all: Bonaparte still would not believe that Austria would be satisfied with a *neutral* Germany.

There was only one way for Napoleon

to test his assessment of Austrian intentions, and that was to see where an assent to negotiations might lead. Hence he at last recognized the neutrality claimed by Metternich and agreed to Austrian mediation, without, however, committing himself to the Reichenbach conditions. An official convention of June 30 confirmed the mediation, provided for a peace conference to open at Prague on July 5, and extended the armistice to August 10. Metternich undertook to make this last acceptable to Prussia and Russia.

Since the extension of the armistice violated the Reichenbach agreement, Metternich had once more to brave the fury of Alexander, Frederick William, Stein,[6] and the rest of the allied camp, whose trust in the Austrian minister now receded from levels that were already near rock bottom. The usual flurry of dispatches and letters from Metternich ensued, on the one hand stressing the need of convincing the Emperor Francis of his son-in-law's recalcitrance, on the other voicing confidence that the negotiations were only a formality and had not the slightest chance of "succeeding."

Yet what Metternich represented to the allies as hopes were in reality his fears. So great was his determination to convince Napoleon of his peaceful intentions that even at this late date he was preparing a revision of the Reichenbach conditions in Napoleon's favor. He realized that he could not further strain the patience of the allies by tampering with the terms that directly concerned them, but he reasoned that they could not object to dropping the one purely Austrian stipulation in the minimal program, the

claim to Illyria, key to the empire's commerce. "The Powers might certainly lay claim to Illyria as a *conditio sine qua non,*" he advised Francis as he made ready for the conference at Prague, "but no one can compel your Majesty to go into a war against your Highness's judgment, for a sacrifice which concerns the monarchy alone." Metternich had no intention of renouncing Illyria forever, since he hoped to obtain the territory later when it was a question of a general, rather than a preliminary peace; but in order to bring about the latter he was resolved to accommodate Bonaparte even on his spiteful vow at Dresden that Illyria was out of the question. To this course Francis agreed, but instructed Metternich to make the concession only "after you have exhausted all other means."

Metternich arrived at Prague on July 12, where he was joined by Baron Johann von Anstett of Russia and Wilhelm von Humboldt of Prussia. The sojourn was a steady succession of disappointments. Metternich found it more difficult than he had supposed to carry out his promise of persuading the allies to accept an extension of the armistice. Since Austria was already committed to enter the war if the armistice expired with the mediation conditions unaccepted, he had no real bargaining power, the more so as news of the great English victory at Vittoria in Spain was just then heartening the allies to resort to arms again. To meet the situation Metternich was compelled to throw in his last reserves. Only by acceding to Alexander's demand that if no peace was signed by August 9 the Russian army would be free to cross the Austrian frontier into Bohemia on the 10th, did he win consent to the extension of the armistice. The last bridge was burned. If France did not acquiesce, there must be war.

---

[6] Frederick William III, King of Prussia; Baron Heinrich Friedrich Karl vom und zu Stein, reform minister of Prussia, 1807–1808, and adviser to the tsar 1812–1814, who favored a German empire — Ed.

Not until the extension had actually been signed (on July 26 at Neumarkt) did Napoleon send an emissary to Prague. The emissary was Armand Caulaincourt and, when he arrived on July 28, he brought, alas, neither a program nor plenary powers but only instructions to sound out the opposition. Nevertheless, the conversations had a constructive side. Although averring in later years that he disdained all discussion until Caulaincourt's credentials arrived, Metternich in fact heard the Frenchman out. Caulaincourt, who personally favored a compromise peace in much the same spirit as did Talleyrand and Fouché,[7] contended that two considerations caused Napoleon's adamant stand. One was the confident belief that Austria, whether from cowardice or from the eastern danger, would under no circumstances fight France; at the most she would remain neutral. The other was the equally firm conviction that the program of the minimum was only the beginning of ever increasing allied demands that would make final peace terms much harsher than those so far broached. Caulaincourt, as a man of peace, implored the Austrian foreign minister candidly to state all his terms, immediately and with sufficient force to convince Bonaparte of Austria's determination to fight. "Demand all that is just and especially whatever contains an idea of a genuine basis of pacification," Caulaincourt urged, and "you will obtain that more easily than a trifle because Napoleon will say: Austria has decided on war rather than a truce; if you ask little of him, he will not make any sacrifice for the peace and he will believe he can make arrangements with you at the expense of the belligerent powers. . . ."

The most striking feature of Caulaincourt's advice was Metternich's complete willingness to follow it. First he stood firm on the armistice, assuring Caulaincourt on July 30, in an oblique allusion to his agreement about the transit of the Russian army, that "beyond the 10th nothing could get the armistice prolonged." The firm stand was apparently successful, for on August 6 Caulaincourt presented a "secret inquiry" from Napoleon himself, who demanded to know "what Austria understood by peace" and whether, in the event that he should accept her terms, Francis would join him in war or merely remain neutral.

The moment for decision had arrived. Austria must now divulge her entire peace program and state her position for or against Napoleon—or risk a separate peace between the flanking powers. A quick trip to Brandeis[8] brought the emperor's approval, and on August 8 Metternich confronted the French emissary with an ultimatum. The first four terms were still the *sine qua non* portion of the Reichenbach pact, to which Austria was irrevocably pledged. But with respect to the two contingent points concerning the Rheinbund and Prussia's restoration, Metternich continued to hedge. Napoleon need only renounce his protectorate, "in order that the independence of all the present sovereigns of Germany be placed under the guarantee of all the powers." The Rheinbund, in short, would not be dissolved. As for the restoration of Prussia, this was to take place "with a tenable frontier on the Elbe," and no mention was made of her 1805 dimensions. These terms Austria was prepared

---

[7] Prince Charles Talleyrand, former foreign minister of Napoleon, and Joseph Fouché, former police minister, both opposed Napoleon's foreign policy at this time.—Ed.

[8] Headquarters of Emperor Francis in Bohemia. —Ed.

to back with her full military power, Metternich said, and demanded an answer "yes or no" by August 10.

In the meantime Metternich had learned from Bubna at Dresden that Napoleon had drafted new instructions for Caulaincourt, containing some concessions but no full consent to any of Austria's demands. But even these had not arrived by August 10 nor had Caulaincourt received his credentials. Anstett and Humboldt, their eyes fastened on the clock, their faces registering the smiles of vindicated prescience, did not wait a minute beyond the stroke of midnight to declare their powers expired. Metternich pronounced the congress dissolved. Whatever his hopes and purposes, he now had no choice but to declare war. Any other course would have cost him his personal prestige, forever impaired his ability to negotiate, and invited a Franco-Russian peace at Austrian expense. Besides, the Austrian army had completed its preparations: it was now ready to play its part. Some idea of what that part would be was indicated on August 6, when Stadion wrested from Alexander a final concession: Schwarzenberg, not the tsar, would command the combined Bohemian army. On August 12 Austria declared war on France.

Metternich devoted but one paragraph in his memoirs to the Congress of Prague —was it a painful experience better minimized for posterity? It is easy to see why it has been commonly described as a farce, a pantomime in which two irreconcilable doctrines, French imperialism and balanced European order, clashed in predetermined futility. Particularly suspicious, of course, was Metternich's sudden *volte face,* which at the last minute added the two contingent Reichenbach terms to the mere *sine qua non* conditions. Superficially the shift gave every appearance of being intended to make peace impossible once Austria's military preparations had been completed—a version that Metternich himself wanted the allies to accept.

Yet this view is outweighed by contrary evidence. First, Metternich proceeded to Prague with the emperor's permission to reduce the terms, not stiffen them, by dropping Illyria from the minimum. Second is the extraordinary similarity between Caulaincourt's advice on July 28 and Metternich's new demands of August 8. Not only were the latter more severe than before, to convince Napoleon of Austria's firmness; but they went beyond the preliminaries to a presentation of Metternich's central ideas for a permanent settlement, no doubt to reassure Bonaparte (again as Caulaincourt advised) that there was a moderate and definable limit to future demands. In this connection the core of the problem continued to be the status of Germany. Even at this late hour Metternich was practicing his guile, offering Napoleon a neutralized Rheinbund under international guarantee while assuring the allies, through Stadion, that he had demanded its dissolution. Similarly, he led them to believe that Prussia's 1805 extent had been demanded.

Did this plan, with its insistence upon "the independence of all the *present* sovereigns of Germany," include Jerome Bonaparte, king of Westphalia? There is no question about it; it was largely for this reason that Prussia must be confined to "a tenable frontier on the Elbe." Thus Metternich's final offer, far from intending to sabotage peace negotiations, was actually a sincere, last-minute plea. It met Austria's own needs. It adumbrated the program he would have pursued at a general peace conference if one had come about: the preservation of the Rheinbund *in toto* to frustrate the Kalisch plans of Prussia and Russia, and the neutralization of the Rheinbund to remove France from Germany and end her European hegemony.

The new formula, like the Kutusov proclamation from Russian headquarters the preceding spring, was non-ideological. Whether a throne was "legitimate" or the fruit of usurpation was of little moment, provided that the territory it ruled was not disposed of contrary to Austria's strategic interests. Only if its system of government made a state the probable pawn of a hostile power did ideological considerations enter Metternich's calculations. This is not to say that he was indifferent to usurpation, that he took revolution with a light heart. He was indeed a conservative. Every man has his political philosophy, more or less articulately worked out, the sort of thing he extolls when addressing his fellow citizens, exhorting his subjects, musing in his study, or giving advice to his son. But in explaining historical causation it is a hazardous leap from abstractions and generalities of this kind to the mainsprings of practical action. With a gifted and complex personality like Metternich the linkage between belief and action is especially devious and tenuous. Throughout his entire career he had to work with slender resources, and he seldom enjoyed the luxury of doing exactly what he willed or willing what he emotionally and morally approved.

In the long years since his flight from the Rhineland Metternich had gradually come to the conclusion that policy and social philosophy operate on two different planes and intersect only at fortuitous intervals. Without panic or overconfidence, without despair or exaltation, he learned how to appraise the new forces abroad in Europe. He learned how to label and catalog them, accept them as

facts to be faced, dangers to be met, tools to be used when trying to influence others, and he learned how to relate them to the old system of international rivalries. Metternich the thinker possibly saw liberalism, democracy, and nationalism as evils; Metternich the diplomat and guardian of Austria's interests saw them only as giving a new dimension to war and diplomacy. The "classical" diplomacy of the eighteenth century had been modified, not invalidated, by the revolutionary age. . . .

The same developments[9] imparted new urgency to the problem of the German constitution. Almost everyone, it seemed, who had ever expressed an opinion on the subject, was present at the new headquarters to add his voice to the excitement of "the Freiburg days." Besides Metternich and Hardenberg there were Stadion and Humboldt, and for Russia Prince Razumovsky and Nesselrode. Gentz,[10] who had remained at Prague sulking over his exclusion from the select company at headquarters, at length received Metternich's summons and arrived on December 15. Stein, delayed by administrative duties at Frankfurt, missed most of the talks but finally appeared on the 20th.

In the generally ebullient atmosphere of Freiburg Metternich found little to relieve his own gloom. True, even the most ardent imperialists had to admit that the middle-state accession treaties had all but eliminated a revival of the Reich, at least in its previous form. But the new plans being circulated in a steady

---

[9] In addition to the above these developments included in the fall of 1813 the defeat of Napoleon at Leipzig, his retreat to the Rhine, and the accession of the German states to the allied cause by treaties which guaranteed their sovereignty. In January 1814, Allied headquarters were in Freiburg. — Ed.

[10] Friedrich von Gentz, publicist and aide to Metternich. — Ed.

effusion of memoranda almost without exception postulated a weak France and made the assumption that Russia would be either benevolent or compliant.

One of the chastened imperialists was Count Stadion. Facing the fact that sovereignty had been promised the middle states, he had reduced his hopes to a confederation consisting of Austria and Prussia and seven or eight middle states, all enlarged by absorption of their smaller neighbors. His primary concern was the defense of the Rhine, for which he considered Stein's plan of joining the fragmented western territories into a union separate from Prussia and Austria wholly inadequate. Nor did he have confidence in a league among equals, which Metternich championed at the time; distant Austria, he claimed, could hardly compete with adjacent France in asserting influence on the Rhine. "Does the ministry in Vienna," he asked, "flatter itself that by its importance and prestige alone it can be effective with these petty sovereigns against all the wiles of human frailty and emotion . . . ? These difficult problems are not yet solved, indeed not yet seriously discussed." To Stadion the only solution was a sweeping rearrangement of territory which would enable the two great powers to overwhelm the lesser states and divide the task of supervising Germany.

Accordingly he desired that Prussia receive Cleve, Berg, Mark, Recklinghausen, Münster, and Westphalia, which would give her control of the Rhine from Mainz to the Dutch border, while Austria would acquire the entire right bank from the Breisgau to Strasbourg, together with a strip of southern Würtemberg to provide a connection with the Austrian crown lands. Should it prove necessary to placate Bavaria, she could be given a place on the middle Rhine and be bound with the two great powers in a special pact to coordinate the defense of Germany's western frontier. The other states, surrounded by Austrian and Prussian territory and cut off from their French protector, would then have no choice but to submit to whatever federal instruments were devised in concert between Berlin and Vienna. The particular federative provisions Stadion considered a routine matter and did not elaborate, except to make it clear that he meant—like the good imperial patriot he was—to include adequate safeguards for the mediatized houses.

Since France was the main target, he was anxious to settle the German question quickly in order to deny her a voice in it. Yet he was not blind to the danger from the East. If defense of the Rhine was uppermost in his plans, it was because France was the present enemy and because he, no less than Metternich, feared a Franco-Russian entente. If anything, he was even more obsessed with it, and therefore he concluded that a strong France would only compound the calamity. Rather than gamble that Bonaparte, even if he could be brought to terms and his throne preserved, would be pro-Austrian and would not attempt to entice the middle states into a new Rheinbund, Stadion preferred the certainty of permanently eliminating at least one of the dangers. Then, and only then, could Austria, from her firm base in Germany and allied to Great Britain and Prussia, concentrate her full strength against Russia, whether in the Balkans, in Poland, or in Germany itself.

Stadion's general conception of the Austrian predicament did not differ fundamentally from that of Metternich. Both strove for a system of collective security in Central Europe. Both attached utmost importance to undertakings with

Britain and Prussia. Since in the winter of 1813–14 these were Austria's most urgent tasks, it is understandable that in the bargaining Metternich should assign Stadion a role second only to his own. They differed, in short, not so much in their schematic representation of the situation as in their assessments of contingencies. Superficially Stadion appeared the greater realist: in his distrust of Napoleon, in his desire to remove the French threat once and for all, in his plea for coercion against the German middle states, and in his readiness to grant Prussia hegemony in North Germany. The program was simple and direct, partly because Stadion was that kind of man, partly because his subordinate position allowed him certain liberties of speculation not available to the responsible policy maker. His realism, in truth, was that of a Felix Schwarzenberg, a Schlieffen, or a Clemenceau: bold, straightforward, decisive, but by these very qualities inflexible, and involving risks the more dangerous for being unperceived rather than calculated.

Such so-called realism has its moments of success, but it commits the often fatal error of being simpler and more direct than reality itself. "Men of this sort," said Metternich of Stadion some years later, "always incline to extremes; for them there are no transitions, and since these nevertheless do exist, when they come before them, instead of knowing how to wait, they often act at random." Stadion understood the need for a rapprochement with Prussia and was lavish in his offers of aggrandizement, yet he stopped short of the one concession necessary for success—Saxony. Regarding the German question as a whole, he perceived that the main problem was how to achieve the acquiescence of the middle states. But when he further argued that coercion must be used and that, if necessary, Austria should threaten a separate peace to bring the tsar to sacrifice his South German relatives, one is at a loss to understand how he still expected to crush France. Stadion's solution of the German problem begged the question. By contrast, Metternich's policy of reconciliation and cooperation with the middle states, though it had its difficulties, was consistent; and it required, as matters stood in December, a minimum of dependence upon the unpredictable decisions of either Napoleon or Alexander. His was the realism of noncommitment, of keeping all roads open as long as possible in the fashion of a Bismarck or a Napoleon. It was not the less realistic for eschewing grand moves on the European chess board; victories are also won by a superior pawn position at the end of the game.

As the preceding selection demonstrates, the difference between Metternich and Stadion constitutes an important subtheme in the controversy over Metternich's policy toward Napoleon. In this context no one has criticized Metternich more cogently than HELLMUTH ROSSLER (1910–1967), late professor at the Technische Hochschule in Darmstadt and the unrivaled master of the archival sources for this period. Rössler's early work in defense of Stadion and other Austrian war hawks exhibited a strong Pan-German bias, which later evolved into nostalgia for the Holy Roman Empire, revival of which was prevented by Metternich's policy of appeasing Napoleon's German satellites. The following selection is from Rössler's fine biography of Stadion, which appeared shortly before his death. In it he implicitly takes account of arguments made against his earlier views.*

Hellmuth Rössler

Unwise Appeaser of France

It is not our task here to describe the shifting diplomatic ups and downs of the summer of 1813 which led to Austria's entry into the war against Napoleon. What interests us is Stadion's part in these events and—since he was only the number-two man in Austrian foreign policy after Metternich—his attitude toward them. More clearly than Stein, who had advised the tsar to extend the defensive war of 1812 to the liberation of Germany, Metternich realized that the tsar-liberator could well go on to set himself up as master of Europe; since the Russo-Prussian alliance of Kalisch, the only way to prevent Russia's threatened dominion over

Germany had been to win over Prussia by satisfying her as completely as possible. More important, however, than detaching Prussian power—which since Tilsit had not been very significant—from the tsar was finding a genuine counterweight to set against him. Metternich counted on England for this; he was all the more shocked, then, when Wessenberg[1] reported to him that the London cabinet had refused to contribute any financial support for Austria's armaments until

---

[1] Baron Johann Philipp von Wessenberg, Austrian diplomat, later Metternich's deputy at the Congress of Vienna.—Ed.

---

*From Hellmuth Rössler, *Graf Johann Philipp Stadion, Napoleons deutscher Gegenspieler* (2 vols.; Vienna and Munich: Herold Verlag, 1966), vol. 2, pp. 79–81, 84–86, 87, 138, 146, omitting most of the original footnotes. Translated by Keith Mostofi and Enno E. Kraehe.

Austria declared herself against Napoleon; England offered £ 20,000 to finance a Tyrolean uprising but rejected mediation by Austria. Wessenberg reported that English egoism had never been so pronounced as now; England would do precisely nothing for a general peace, as her policy would be based on war as long as she was concerned exclusively with monopolizing sea trade. People in London spoke of the war in Germany as they would of a war in India. When Metternich sent Wessenberg's report on to Stadion and added that the entire account revealed the anti-Continental bias of the London cabinet, Stadion replied ironically that apparently neither Metternich nor Wessenberg realized that England was only halfway a European power. As Wessenberg saw it, England relied on the alliance she had concluded with Russia to prevent any political unification of the Continent. Metternich endeavored all the harder to maintain a counterweight to Russia in Napoleon, whom he hoped to bring around to a voluntary renunciation of his control over Germany east of the Rhine. Metternich hoped to extort this concession without war by means of Austria's mediation backed up by the army; accordingly, he spread word abroad of Emperor Francis' desire for peace. From this, all European diplomats learned, as Stadion and the other Austrian leaders already knew, that now, just as when Stadion had directed foreign policy, the emperor was entrusting himself to whoever was his foreign minister of the moment, since, so he believed, the only political terrain completely familiar to him was internal administration. What a lack of insight into human nature for such a glittering social figure as Metternich to believe that Napoleon would sign a peace involving sacrifices, that he would abandon the still intact system of the Confederation of the Rhine without resort to the sword! Metternich believed that he would, but this faith was no longer justified after his conversation with Napoleon in the Marcolini Palace in Dresden on June 26, 1813. When Metternich told Napoleon on this occasion that peace, war, and the destiny of Europe were in his hands and that for the preservation of peace he must retire to limits consistent with general repose, Napoleon answered him abruptly, "Well then, what do people want me to do? To bring disgrace to myself? Never! I will know how to die, but I am not surrendering an inch of territory. Rulers who are born to the throne can be defeated twenty times and always return to their capitals; a child of fortune like me cannot do that. My reign will not survive the day I cease to be strong and people stop fearing me." In spite of this Metternich held fast to his idea for peace. Although Cauliancourt himself told him he should present harsh terms because only then would Napoleon believe in Austria's final resolve, he continually moderated the conditions for peace. . . .

The . . . interview with Napoleon in Dresden on June 26 brought Metternich no success although he reduced his terms for peace unconditionally. Napoleon was not even prepared to pull back to the Lübeck-Trieste line as part of the peace. Nevertheless, Metternich still held firmly to the hope that Napoleon might come around, as he had in very general terms declared himself ready for a conference in Prague in July. So in return Metternich granted him an extension of the armistice until August 10. Again he was fooled, because although Cauliancourt arrived as Napoleon's representative, he was without full powers or instructions. Metternich's attitude did not change even when news came, during the Prague congress, that Wellington had defeated the French army at Vittoria and that the French were retreating from Spain. Right at the start of the congress, he showed his willingness to facilitate peace by giving up Austria's demand for Illyria. Two days before the expiration of the armistice, he scaled down his demands still further: he did not demand the dissolution of the Confederation of the Rhine, only Napoleon's abandonment of his protectorate, so that the princes of the Confederation, even the Bonapartes in Berg and Westphalia, would become independent under a guarantee of all the powers; the restoration of Prussia was to mean now only a defensible frontier on the Elbe without reference to Prussia's territorial extent in 1806. But even here Metternich was frustrated; Napoleon made no reply. On August 10, Austria had no choice but to enter the war against Napoleon.

One can admire Metternich's desire for peace and justify it in terms of the profound state of exhaustion in which Austria found herself: since 1792 she had been at war for a total of nine years, far longer than had Russia or Prussia, which altogether had fought for only four years against the Revolution and Napoleon. Nevertheless, it was obvious that, now or never, the moment had come to win Austria's independence, and this could only be accomplished with the liberation of Prussia and Germany. Metternich, who constantly placed the European balance of power in the forefront of his calculations, must have had to tell himself that even the preservation of Austria's independence would be meaningless if Napoleon evacuated merely the territory east of the Lübeck-Trieste line; Austria would still remain diplomatically weak, and effective rehabilitation of her finances could not be achieved with such paltry territorial acquisitions. Also, with Metternich's Lübeck-Trieste line, the power

of Austria and Prussia would have remained so circumscribed that it would not have sufficed to provide a barrier between Napoleon and Russia; the expectation of being able to reinforce this barrier by adding a neutralized Confederation of the Rhine could not be based on any available evidence. Did Metternich actually believe that he would be able to bind the princes of the Confederation to Austria in the face of all the personal and political influence and bribes of Napoleon and the tsar? This was not accomplished later, even at the high point of success against Napoleon. Who was to prevent an alliance between him and the tsar?[2]

In July 1813 Metternich told Emperor Francis that in less than four years Austria had regained preeminence in Europe. He gave credit for this above all to the emperor, who alone in 1809 had kept his courage when all the resources of the monarchy lay in ruins and every minister regarded the demise of the state in peace or war as inevitable. Of himself, Metternich spoke only with polite modesty: aided by fortunate circumstances and the confidence of the emperor, he had done what duty and conscience had demanded of him. The emperor answered the way Metternich had expected: "I have you, in large part, to thank for the present glorious political condition of my monarchy." The speech and the reply contained only half-truths. The inability of Austria to fight on anew in 1809 was due not to the destruction of all the resources of the monarchy but to the emperor's lack of resolution. Stadion had expected the collapse of

---

[2] These criticisms and apprehensions on Stadion's part are to be found especially in his reports of May 27 and June 2, 1913. . . . Here, as in the whole judgement of Metternich's position in the summer of 1813, the interpretations of H. von Srbik and Kraehe suffer from the fact that both of them in their extensive efforts did not use Metternich's reports of 1813. . . .

the monarchy only in the sense that a prolonged association with Napoleon's dominion would have lost Austria her independence and any real existence as a state. That Napoleon's great attack on Russia would miscarry, only Baldacci, the emperor's cabinet councillor, had believed, not Metternich; but it was to this failure alone that Austria owed the reconquest of her independence. One could maintain that she had assumed the leading role in Europe only if one did not count Russia, or England, or France. Again, the policy of armed mediation which Metternich now carried out, and which finally proved successful with Austria's entry into the war and Napoleon's defeat, was not original with Metternich but was Stadion's plan of 1807, while Metternich's strength—and weakness—lay only in his diplomatic execution of it.

In this Metternich confirmed the judgment of Gentz, who now admired him: "not a man of great passion or bold impulses, not a genius, but a great talent; cool, calm, imperturbable, and a calculator *par excellence.*" One might say that he was not a man of great goals and political creativity but a man of method, theory, and system. Count Ernst Hardenberg, representative of Hanover to Vienna, had viewed Metternich as early as in 1812 as a statesman who had done absolutely nothing for the internal recovery of Austria, but had merely used his one success—the marriage of Marie Louise to Napoleon—for the safety of Austria: "With a high opinion of the superiority of his gifts . . . he loves finesse in politics and considers it a necessity. Since he does not have enough energy to make use, where necessary, of the resources of the country . . ." he is inclined to substitute cunning for character, courage, and strength and—if that does not work—to yield for the moment in hopes of extricating himself from embarrassment by some new ruse.

We come now to Stadion's contrary position. In the middle of June 1813, a rumor spread through Vienna that the emperor had appointed Stadion foreign minister in place of Metternich. When this report proved incorrect, the general morale sank noticeably—a factor not without its importance for the quotations of government bonds and the new currency. To be sure, Stadion's recall would have been in line with the thoughts that not only he but also the emperor and Metternich had had at the time of Stadion's voluntary resignation in the autumn of 1809. But Metternich was not a man to depart voluntarily as Stadion had done, and he was sufficiently a master of intrigue to be able to stifle at its source any thought the emperor might have had concerning a change of ministers. Precisely because of the way the emperor, under Metternich's influence, desired peace at any price, Stadion's contrary views had to antagonize him.

In the headquarters of the Allies, of course, Stadion's attitude was from the start the one that gained the greatest sympathy for Austria. . . . Stadion saw it as his mission during Austria's mediation maneuver to prepare for her switchover to the Allies and to the war against Napoleon. In contrast to Metternich, he considered Napoleon's acquiescence in a peace involving even the mildest concessions as incompatible not only with his character but also with the interests of Austria, Germany, and Europe. From the start, therefore, he had the distasteful task of playing a double game: in Vienna and with the Austrian army, to strengthen the will to fight; with the Allies, not to allow their confidence in Austria's future participation to waver and to bring about a unity among them. . . .

Today one is inclined to admire Metternich's superior wisdom in his generous treatment of France, especially since in the twentieth century, democratically governed states have dictated peace terms aimed at the dismemberment and permanent weakening of other states, without holding to the new international law they themselves have proclaimed. In fact, Metternich's conduct toward France in 1814, as in 1815, was understanding and tolerant because he did not allow himself to be influenced by feelings of revenge or national sentiment. As the advocate of European equilibrium, he wanted to gain a strong France as partner in an alliance against a dangerously threatening Russia. Nevertheless, his calculations were soon shattered. While a close relationship with the restored Bourbons never came about, Metternich found himself joined with the Russians in a Holy Alliance of conservative character. Despite this indulgent treatment, France did not reconcile herself to the Vienna treaties, and even if the Bourbons and later the House of Orléans were able for so long to curb the desire for revenge in the bourgeoisie and the army, this desire broke through in the end. It took another war, the one of 1870–1871, to destroy France's hopes for revenge, for the reconquest of the entire left bank of the Rhine, and for the blocking of German unity. In 1848, 1859, and 1866, France stood against Austria, favoring Prussia instead. . . .

From the European standpoint, Stadion viewed Germany as a *force intermédiaire* but—and in this he differed from his mentor Kaunitz, on the basis of his experience over the last ten years—as a central power of an active type; Metternich's idea that Germany was to serve as a merely passive buffer separating the great flanking powers seemed unrealistic to Stadion. He had to combat it, because he regarded Austria and Prussia as active partners in the European equilibrium while at the same time correctly recognizing their dependence upon and their natural interest in the resources of Germany. If this was true, the exercise of mere diplomatic influence by the two leading German powers on the middle and small states could satisfy neither their needs nor those of Europe. Only a durable influence could have assured the two great German powers of the existence of the nation on whom they depended, and could have made this nation the guarantor of the security and freedom of Europe. To that extent there remained alive in Stadion's thinking—as everywhere—the basic ideas he had absorbed in his youth, the words from "Letters of Two Canons": "The German must become aware of and feel what his duty is: namely, to be the guardian of the European constitution and the savior of humanity against recurring despotism. The princes can do this if they let the humblest of people experience Germanic freedom. They must do this, or they will perish because they wish to have the ends without the means." Stadion had wanted to do this, but was defeated. Austria, whose preeminent significance for Europe we recognize today just as clearly as Talleyrand did in 1805, lost, through Metternich's diplomacy, the power to guarantee the equilibrium and thus to preserve the freedom of Europe.

HEINRICH RITTER VON SRBIK (1878–1951) held the chair of modern history at the University of Vienna from 1922 to 1945. His brilliant lectures and many erudite books stressed the German character of Austria and the need for Austro-German union. Generally, however, he is best known for his massive two-volume biography *Metternich der Staatsmann und der Mensch* (Munich, 1925), which is still the most important single work on Metternich. In it he argues that Metternich was not the narrow and reactionary Austrian opportunist commonly depicted but a constructive European statesman guided by enlightened and coherent principles. The work stimulated so much new research that a third volume (published posthumously in 1954) was necessary to comment on this output. Srbik discusses the ideas behind "the Metternich system" both in the biography and, in shorter form, in an article in Germany's leading historical journal. The latter provides the selection used here.*

Heinrich Ritter von Srbik

Statesman of Philosophical Principles

Today there can no longer be any doubt that Metternich's diplomatic ability towered far above the ordinary, but he was no Richelieu or Mazarin and could not back his political finesse with the weight of a powerful state. Therefore, the prime explanation of his political significance must be sought in the strength of the political idea he represented. This idea, the "Metternich system," cannot have been simply the outer dressing for what was actually a nucleus of power and political egoism, a deceptive politics of convenience which concealed the realism underneath; for mere realism in false dress could not have held the conflicting interests of state together for so long a time. The interest of his particular state, which was no doubt a factor with Metternich as with any statesman, must have been combined with a force making for unity among states; his ideas must have possessed an unusually wide appeal which had its roots in the temper of the times. These ideas must have been European in nature. "For a long time now Europe has had for me the quality of a fatherland"—as he himself described his supranational thought to Wellington in 1824. Metternich's system was far more than

*From Heinrich Ritter von Srbik, "Der Ideengehalt des 'Metternichschen Systems,'" *Historische Zeitschrift*, CXXXI (1925), 241–262. Translated by Keith Mostofi and Enno E. Kraehe.

mere diplomatic phraseology. Historiography has the duty of comprehending the content of his thought, undeterred by love or hatred.

Contemporaries and posterity have uttered the phrase "Metternich system" thousands of times and have often defined it simply as a system of immobility. They have fixed on the tone of didactic, moralizing pedantry, the bland abstract form which over the years became more and more the hallmark of the chancellor's statements, and they have turned with rage and bitterness against the consequences of the "system." The "System" cried out against the old chancellor on the judgment day of his life, March 13, 1848, and the curse against the system pursued him beyond the grave. He himself never wanted to acknowledge in his personal work anything like a system. As time went on it became his firm conviction that his political principles were nothing other than old-fashioned understanding, the laws governing progression from the bad to the good and from the good to the better. He imputed to these ideas a timeless and suprapersonal significance; he refrained from advocating a speculative complex of preconceived doctrines divorced from the real world and rejected the expression "system" on the grounds that preconceived systems were only obstacles to statesmanlike action, the sterile games of idle heads. And accustomed to differentiating, to indulging in antithesis, he set forth his convictions as *principles*, as opposed to systems or doctrines. The practical sense of a statesman rebelled against purely rationalistic constructions of the brain. Nevertheless, his principles seemed to him to be eternal truths, a world order that anyone with a sound mind and a sincere heart could understand.

He never realized how much of the doctrinaire his principles contained. He believed he was avoiding a priori arbitrariness, and he did in fact, in the "practical logic" that he claimed for himself, indissolubly combine realism (which he possessed like any important politician) with the constant effort to use the laws of logic to reduce the whole range of mental and natural phenomena to general principles in terms of which to explain the phenomena. He was wrong in opposing the expression system, and when he objected to the term Metternich system he was in the right only insofar as he was the main advocate of its teachings, though by no means its exclusive creator.

In this connection I can only point out that one can discern in Metternich's being from the time of his youth, an exceedingly strong impulse to search beyond the phenomena of the mental and physical world for lawlike regularities and then in the factual realm to test them empirically and experimentally and prove them right; to give precedence to deductive theory, and to phenomena only the role of providing a field of observation. He manifested this proclivity in dealing with organic and inorganic nature just as with society and its highest organization, the state. The consistency of his ideas throughout his entire life is quite extraordinary. Just as there is relatively little transforming development discernible in his intellectual makeup after reaching maturity, just as the politics of perseverance and preservation had their intimate first cause in his own tendency to rest, so did his tendency to apprehend the world through reason only grow stronger with increasing age, and more solidified by the events of time. The intellectual makeup of the young man and the old differ only in degree; a sharp division in Metternich before and after 1815, as has indeed been sought, does not exist. He remained a born system-maker until his death; only his formulation of principles became ever broader and more detailed, ever more didactic and colorless, until at last, to an age estranged from him, the principles looked entirely like some quaint impossibility or an illusion, half familiar, half unknown. However, Metternich's system never became political cant. He did not invent "the right," as Sorel[1] claimed; his convictions did not come after the fact, as others thought; rather, his system was the expression of a firmly rooted ideal, the ideal of reaction—in the scientific sense, not as moralizing; it was the countermove against the doctrine of the Great Revolution, sprung from an inner desire working outward toward the rationalizing of action, as Karl Gross[2] recently said, at its depths lying in the century of his birth, and brought to maturity by the most convulsive events.

Metternich was truly the last major statesman who conducted policy in the rational and systematic spirit of the Age of Reason, the last who in an age of aggressive realism still could say that by his nature he had to repudiate any political course that did not rest on a foundation of principle and who could speak of his *philosophie gouvernementale;* the last mellow product of an epoch in which a "philosopher-king"[3] was at the same time an eminently practical politician who sought the universal beyond the flux of phenomena and combined empiricism with the philosophy of Locke and Voltaire. He was the spiritual offspring of an age in which the great king's greatest political opponent, Kaunitz, after the collapse of his practical political system,

wrote as a theorist on substituting justice and sanctity of treaties for convenience and force; on freedom and equality and their limitation in the interests of the whole; and on the necessity of repose, order, and authority. Too, Kaunitz wanted to practice politics on the basis of reason alone; he regarded politics as a science that could be taught, and in the end he arrived at a universal doctrine of humanity. Did not the art of war before Clausewitz[4] also pass through a comparable stage? Was not Joseph II in every realistic political sense a doctrinaire believer in natural law? And did not the Great Revolution overthrow the old order of state and society with genuine doctrinaire principles? Metternich was not the only systematizer of the state and social order prominent in the new century. What inspiring harmony exists between the ideas of the European-minded statesman Metternich and the Prussian Ancillon![5] Wangenheim,[6] the advocate of the idea of German trialism, built on the philosophical teachings of a contemporary at Tübingen; and it was remarked, probably correctly, even of that determined opponent of ideology, Napoleon, that in the years of the Empire he was no longer guided by practical circumstances alone but followed a system, a method, in his thinking and action.

Metternich's system exhibits in what it affirms and what it rejects the rich heritage of prerevolutionary French philosophy and political and social doctrines. Of lasting effect also was the influence

---

[1] Albert Sorel, French historian.—Ed.
[2] See p. 48.—Ed.
[3] The allusion is to Frederick the Great of Prussia. —Ed.

[4] Karl von Clausewitz, famous Prussian writer on the theory of war.—Ed.
[5] Johann Peter Friedrich Ancillon, Prussian diplomat and foreign minister.—Ed.
[6] Baron Karl August von Wangenheim, Württemberg diplomat who advocated "trialism," that is, a separate union of the medium and small states in Germany.—Ed.

of the teachers of Metternich's youth:
Koch, the Strasbourg instructor in international law, and the historian Vogt, of
Mainz, who implanted in him the view
that states exist as a family, bound in
solidarity and arranged in equilibrium.
To this was unmistakably joined the intellectual impact of Burke and—as odd
as this may at first sound—the Kantian
critical philosophy of reason and morality
as the basis of human culture; the rejection of the polarity between politics and
morality, the erection of an international
law under the impetus of justice—these
too were taken over. It may have been
through the Kantian, Bouterwek,[7] and his
doctrine of virtualism that there was reinforced in Metternich the assumption of
two opposing forces whose union produced absolute reality and whose balance
was the basis of the world order. The
significance of the young Metternich's
studies in natural science and medicine
becomes more tangible. He always took
on himself the parallel pursuit of natural
science and political and social science;
he often drew comparisons between the
art of government and chemistry or
pathology, and it could be demonstrated
to what extent Metternich believed that
Brown's theory of agitation[8]—which he
picked up from Peter Frank, the founder
of the "medical police," and accepted as valid for the individual human
body—could also be applied to the *corps
social.* Here we must be satisfied with in-
dicating what an exceedingly strong impact the organic combination of natural
science and philosophy made on his

thought, in particular his political and social doctrines. Essentially, a natural rationalism, combined with natural empiricism, influenced his conception of the
world more than did the historicism of the
Enlightenment.

Only secondary importance in Metternich's system can be assigned to Haller's[9] basically rationalistic conservatism.
And as much as the idea of the continuity
of all historical life, the appreciation of
historically given peculiarities and variations, the denial of man's capacity to
create, and the doctrine of natural becoming—as much as these connect Metternich
with romanticism, he (who even in his religious life never lost the heritage of rationalism) never occupied the same plane
with specifically romantic religiosity;
he never equated his concept of organism
with that held by romanticism; he always
remained pledged to an ultimately mechanistic, quantitative, and calculable cau-
sality.

Much in his fund of ideas was conveyed
to him through intercourse with intellectual giants like Wilhelm von Humboldt[10]; much stemmed from voracious
reading; in many ways his schoolmaster
was Friedrich von Gentz, whose practical
political influence on Metternich was
meager; yet for all that, the intellectual
assets of the statesman himself were by no
means slender. Independently and in
common with Gentz he held his whole
life long to the idea of the European balance of power, the valuation of the historically given state above the nation, the
high esteem for strong authority as
against the blind crowd, the aversion to
everything loud and violent, and a deep

---

[7] Friedrich Bouterwek, Göttingen philosopher
and founder of "absolute virtualism," a theory which
holds that we perceive reality by means of the will.
—Ed.

[8] That is, the so-called Brownian movement of a
particle suspended in a fluid, a phenomenon named
after the Scottish botanist Robert Brown.—Ed.

[9] Karl Ludwig von Haller, Swiss theorist who held
that the state was the private property of the ruling
prince.—Ed.

[10] Prussian diplomat, minister of education,
scholar, and liberal reformer.—Ed.

anxiety about the dissolution of the traditional social order.

The role of Emperor Francis in the second, that is, the empirical, side of the system is only indirect. In this regard the prime governing force was the great experience of the Revolution and the Empire. If the Revolution showed Metternich where the unrestrained mass can lead state and society under the banner of natural-law theories arrived at deductively, the work of the man who completed, tamed, and triumphed over the Revolution demonstrated a technique for gaining mastery over the ideas of 1789. Napoleon's enlightened despotism, which Hegel and Alexander I also admired, showed how the state, in an atmosphere of absolute order and objectivity, would keep individualism within bounds. Napoleon, the man who scorned popular sovereignty, parliamentary oratory, and freedom of the press, who made light of individual liberty and the "people," the man of authoritarianism in legislative and administrative matters—he set the pattern for a system of regulating all collective and individual factors in society for the good of the state and for the guidance, supervision, and suppression of the press; this same Napoleon who regarded Italians as unsuited to unity and liberty and who prized religion and the church as forces for preserving society. Other factors at work on the empirical side of the system were the ever-growing social and national upward pressure of the people who were weary of the old authorities and yearned to determine their own fate, individual acts of violence, and secret leagues and revolutions, all of which, in the final analysis, led back to the great upheaval in France.

The unity of the Metternich system corresponds to the unity of Metternich's political life; its core, the preservation of the historical order of things, remained always the same. Metternich himself divided his life into the political period, lasting until 1813, 1815, or 1816/17, and the social, lasting until his overthrow. This consistency arose for him from the consistency of his adversary, the revolutionary idea, which varied only in appearance, and from the unalterable nature of his principles. The struggle against Napoleon was political in nature and served to reconstruct the historical state system; then, with growing force, the struggle for the historical social order came into the foreground. In this sense Metternich could characterize himself as a born socialist, that is, as a politician of society. He saw it as his mission, as his apostolate, to do battle with the demon of the *demos* in Europe, as Kübeck put it. To the fact and theory of social revolution and social evolution he opposed the fact and theory of social preservation. Metternich's fixed universalist belief forms the backbone of the fully developed system; it is aimed at regulating "the social field over a broader area than that contained within the boundaries of a state." In this social-conservative idea of the system the idea of the national state is definitively rejected.

These are the premises from which I propose to undertake a quick survey of the most important programmatic ideas of the system. Metternich himself never systematically collected them into a whole, but from thousands of his precepts one can reconstruct without any forcing the edifice of his world, state, and social outlook as a whole.

At the top stands the theory of the dualism of the spiritual (moral) and the material (natural) worlds. In both worlds eternal, opposing forces (powers) are active. The moral powers are converted into material; the eternal opposition of the spiritual forces calls forth the movement of the natural. The psychic and natural forces are governed by eternal moral laws, unquestionably recognizable to the intellect and constituting a God-given moral order; the material forces, however, are additionally controlled by the laws of nature: by the law of gravity, of attraction and repulsion, of chemical combination and disintegration. Following the same fixed moral and natural rules are the forces, or "powers," in humanity, which consists of both psychic and physical components and forms a great social entity composed of such elements as states, churches, hereditary estates, and individuals. Life consists of a perpetual antagonism and reciprocating action of the opposing forces, which form a unity only as idea. The most dominant of these forces are those of persistence and movement, the positive and the negative, the conserving and the destroying principles. If material forces are set in motion by the conflict of moral powers, their struggle knows no bounds or limit; they battle until the defeat of the one or the other. For the existence of the individual, society, and the whole of nature, an equilibrium of forces is necessary. An absolute and enduring equilibrium contradicts the nature of life as movement, but it is an ideal which must be striven for, because the life and death of society depend on the greatest possible paralyzing of the grinding struggle of the dualistic extremes.

We recognize here the age-old belief in the conflict of hostile basic principles; we recognize Holbach's law of attraction and repulsion; we are reminded of Herder's doctrine of the culture-building and culture-destroying forces; we compare Kant's precritical doctrine that matter originates from the reciprocal functioning of the attractive and repulsive forces, and Kant's view that nature wills not concord but discord, that the generation of human energies proceeds from the antagonism of effective principles and the just state combines freedom and necessary constraint. We think of Vogt's theory of equilibrium, of Bouterwek's transcendental realism, and Gentz's famous positing of the two principles constituting the moral and intelligible world, that of perpetual progress and that of the necessary limitation of this progress, of their happy balance in the best ages of the world, and of the necessity of conservatism to the point of obstinacy for counteracting the destructive tendency. We recognize the age-old core of ideas also in Adam Müller's[11] philosophy of opposition and his conception of the state as a union of past, present, and future generations in which contemporaries embody the principle of movement, while the successive inhabitants of a given territory represent the principle of continuity and repose. And did not the young Hegelians, as has recently been said, turn Hegel's dialectic back from the metaphysical into the realistic and "assume two polarized forces in the social organism which stand to each other in the relationship of thesis and antithesis and by their mutual negation bring forth historical progress as their product"? "In opposition to the positive, which one can characterize as the sum of the preserving forces in the life of the state" they have "set the aggregate of the forward-striving forces as the negative" and in the continual alternations, in the constant progression toward negation, they have seen development in history taking place. We find these ideas again in the historical materialism of Karl Marx.

The system is a defensive system: it aims at protecting the old international law against the new, the old social order

---

[11] Conservative German writer in Austrian service. — Ed.

against the revolution. It is fundamentally neither retrograde nor stationary in principle, has nothing to do with reaction or with permanent stability, but, with due regard for the lightning pace of the destructive principle, desires only to let the course of the conserving principle proceed in measured steps, in a "logical, natural order of serial development"; what the system rejects is experimentation and the erratic alteration of existing things. Master of antithesis, Metternich distinguished between stability and immobility; he wanted to undertake change only in a legal fashion after mature consideration, to protect innovation that had been legally produced or subsequently legalized, to obstruct only rash and hasty demolition, to protect the eternal principles of reason and morality from utopias ·and whims, and to stand firm on the ground of a political and social order based on law.

The victorious advance of an unrestrained destructive principle is to be checked by a double system of relative balance, or, to put it better, of counterweights: the system of *political* counterweights insures the existence and equal rights of the political entities within the great family of states; the counterpart of this political or external balance is the internal or *social* equilibrium, the balance between the middle class, bent on destruction and innovation, on one side, and a strong first estate and the materially contented masses, on the other. The result is relative calm in the political and social field.

This repose is always a necessity of existence for the social body as a whole, for its component organizations, and for individual men. For the physical natures and psyches of these are changeless in essence; only the forms change. The psychical and spiritual nature of states and peoples and the importance of climate, soil characteristics, and insular or continental location—these remain constant. Any healthy human community, like the normal individual, passes through its childhood, youth, adulthood, and old age; its spirit and its body live on in altered conditions. The social body moves in a circle; fundamentally there is nothing new under the sun; the events of the present are only variations, not themes. Only sins against the two sovereign lords of human destiny—moral laws and natural laws—lead states, peoples, and society to sickness and death by suicide, and even then the basic elements are not lost.

A line of development leads from Polybius, Plato, and the Stoics through Machiavelli, Frederick the Great, Herder, and Johannes von Müller to Heinrich Leo,[12] Gentz, and Metternich, indeed all the way to Bismarck and to Oswald Spengler, if we pursue this conception of the cycle of human nature and of the fate of nations and states and of the stages in the life of peoples in the history of mind; the role of climate and soil leads back to Montesquieu and Herder, and the doctrine of the unchangeable nature of men and peoples to Voltaire and Herder.

Among the factors making up the totality of humanity, the system, with its ungenetic outlook, assigns full weight only to the supernational communities, the "races," and states founded in history. The individualities of which the great social combine, society, is composed are political bodies; the individual nations are not conceived of as such. All states exist in a community of interests transcending the individual units and resting on their common quality as parts of society.

The political equilibrium is realized, within the limits of the attainable, by the

---

[12] Müller and Leo were German historians.—Ed.

new order of Europe following the age of the universal despot. The state system is restored; it rests on the federative principle, and in it both force and the egoism and preponderance of any single state are sharply curbed by the principles of solidarity and reciprocity. Here one sees the last expression of the old international law, which seeks to restrain the vital instincts of peoples, their immanent demands for expansion and power, by the tenets of international morality and the doctrine of the unity of a confederated Europe. The state is not an end in itself like the pure power-state and not a fully autonomous organism, but is bound by the eternal moral order and the idea of justice. It is part of a universal. That idea of solidarity and reciprocity is now carried further in its peculiar way into the social realm. After the reconstruction of the political body of Europe comes the task of the reconstruction of the social body, and this duty falls on the political pentarchy of the five great powers joined together as a moral pentarchy—in the internal affairs of states once the international have been arranged. The unity of the five is the remedy for turbulence, the only salvation in the struggle between the old and the new *ordre social.*

Just as in the political system of equilibrium, so also in the social, the small states have to accommodate themselves entirely to the great leaders, voluntarily or by coercion. If an action of the pentarchy in the social sphere becomes necessary, then, with a complete moral solidarity, the roles can be allotted according to the proximity of a member to the site of the revolution and other practical considerations. The right of intervention, one must acknowledge, is justified as a self-evident consequence of the solidarity of society. Its second justification, besides the general European, is that of the individual state's interest in repose, the duty of self-preservation, which has to take into account the fact that social bodies, like material ones, find themselves constantly adjusting their temperature to their environment.

Vitally necessary order and repose can be preserved in the struggle of forces only by a superimposed power; otherwise anarchy would result. The urge to association lies in the basic condition of mankind; every association, from the social community above the state down to the club, can fulfill its purpose only by rules that protect the urge to association (in itself an expression of the creative principle) against degenerating into the crippling and destroying principle. Without authority there is no order; without order, no freedom. In this the system resembles the teachings of Locke and Montesquieu. There cannot be true freedom without an order-creating and order-maintaining legal power; order can be built with certainty only upon the monarchical principle, which is based, above all other things, on right and strength, in order to control competing ideas and material movements, to protect what legally exists, and to direct the natural step-by-step advance. It is in this unique capacity of the sovereign crown to exercise the "supreme right of guardianship" that the most profound justification of the monarchical principle lies, not in legitimacy in the sense of a prince's hereditary rights. As far as the system is concerned, princely legitimacy has always been merely the means to carry out the higher ideal, never a central dogma, as people so often have thought. From the beginning of his political activity, Metternich, in opposition to Gentz, regarded the principle of legitimacy only as something "conceived in time and modifiable with time," not as an absolute or one of the eternal principles.

He was capable of feeling strong sympathy for the office of president of the United States. It is the indivisible sovereign authority for whose unalterable necessity the system stands. For Metternich, legitimacy was the best, but not the only possible basis for monarchy. Legitimacy is a part of the overall positive legal order and an especially important part, but not a "principle," and the enemy is not so much illegitimacy in itself as the uncontrolled movement usually allied with it, the tendency to disorder and blind destruction.

In the legal and social realm, this destructive tendency finds its strongest expression in the idea of popular sovereignty, in which the system sees the buds of eighteenth-century individualism and humanitarianism. Like a delirium, there swept over humanity the doctrine of the separation of powers, of the natural equality and liberty of mankind, of human and civil rights, and the desire for leveling, only in the end to put the have-nots in the place of the haves, to destroy the custodians of morality and material property, and to terminate with disenchantment. At no point does the system in its entirety become so clearly a reaction against the democratic principle of the Great Revolution as in the antithesis between the monarchical principle, with its individual power of princely sovereignty, on the one hand, and popular sovereignty, with separation of powers, on the other, and in the antithesis between leveling and natural differentiation, between authority and anarchy, between historical right and revolutionary ideology.

The system makes no concession in questions of principle. It is one of its chief characteristics that it knows only a blunt either-or: "pure monarchy" or popular sovereignty in the form of a republic— as the expression of two eternally hostile forces; no synthesis, no *juste milieu*. A monarchy on representative foundations is an absurdity, something incomplete, an artificial device that puts the crown in the shadows, makes the throne a wooden armchair, and leads to rule by factions and demagogues. In truth, for the Continent, whose life circumstances are different from those of England and America, none but those two opposite political forms is proper: no toying with that French novelty, the charter, or with any constitution that has not developed naturally and has only the times to thank for what it is! Trying to create a constitution means producing a revolution by legislative means; strife, idle babbling, corruption, and autocracy at the hands of the people's seducers are the practical result of creating popular representative bodies. Once they exist on a legal basis, however, they can be divested of their most dangerous features, that is, publicizing their proceedings and ministerial responsibility, not by a *coup d'état* from above but only by legal means.

A "pure monarchy" is not to be confused with monarchical despotism or even with bureaucratic absolutism. It is a *monarchie temperée:* the monarch may not transgress the laws; he is bound by the law as an emanation of the moral order of the world. The check on the arbitrariness of the monarch in legislative, executive, and judicial functions, which of course lie in his hands, is reason and the moral law derived from it, which teaches the wearer of the crown to obey the existing public and private law and to develop it only in conformity with nature. As even Kaunitz had demanded, a guardian of reason, morality, and law—a council whose task is to see to the preservation of the law, public and private—should stand at the monarch's side. In other words, the ruler should run his government in the council, not from his private study; he should share actual power and responsibility with the council.

So much for the top of the state. The *good* state is created on the concrete foundations of its nature and history, the irrational impulses of the national character, and the customs, habits, and wishes of the people; it is not created according to some natural-law model. It safeguards the material interests of the subjects, their civil rights, and their individual freedom within the framework of the legal order; and it checks the despotism of the mob. The ordering power is sovereign; the exercise of sovereignty means governing; the people cannot govern themselves since governing is the opposite of obeying. Who would do the obeying if the masses governed?

The system is obviously still far removed from seeing in the state a personality of its own, separated from people and authority, and equally far from the conception of the state as the living embodiment of the people. The state is a form of social organization. In the eyes of the system the ideal state is diametrically opposed to Rousseau's farfetched natural-law doctrine of contract and to a leveling and atomizing rationalism. The political thought of the system is collective in nature, like that of Joseph II or Frederick II, and also rationalistic. Rationalistically the state is founded on the necessity of association and on practical good sense: this state is not there for the individual and his free development; its function is not the moral education of the citizen and the development of the political energies of the community through the *ethos* of the free personality; this state is alien to the idea of humanity, alien to Kant's idea of right and the ethical socialism of Fichte, alien to Hegelian metaphysics. Its purpose is the order and repose of the

social organism in the eternal cycle of things. Preserved in this doctrine of the state are numerous vestiges of the mechanistic outlook of Schlözer and other political philosophers of the eighteenth century. With German political romanticism it shares an affinity with Burke, the rejection of Montesquieu, Rousseau, and natural law; and like romanticism it shuns constitutional stereotypes, singles out the unique in nature and history, and accordingly stands close to the *Volksgeist* doctrine and the organic ideas of romanticism; in fact, however, romanticism is much more an ally than an essential source. . . . All in all this is the prerevolutionary idea of necessity and utility reshaped by the social experience of the revolutionary period, which had proved how indispensable the state was for maintaining order against the irrational mass.

Likewise rationalistic and empirical in this state, which treats subjects as mute creatures, is the evaluation, from the standpoint of public order, of the separate hereditary classes as historically given forms of social organization. The system does not, like Baron Stein, aim at conferring equal political rights on the separate social estates and so combining them into an integral society in the state and for the state; it does not, like Haller, try to break state and society down into a series of separate units and districts with essentially private-law powers; it does not, like romanticism, integrate organically the diverse and peculiar in the living structure of nature into the great community of society; rather, without hard-and-fast compartmentalizing, it treats social groups first and foremost according to their preserving or destructive effects. Without assigning to them specific shares of work to be performed for the state—as, say, under the enlightened autocracy of Frederick the Great—but on the other hand without recognizing a general citizenry and civil rights, the system sees in an ordered hierarchy a basic condition for order in society. It is the function of the nobility as a social corporation to form natural buffer groups between crown and people, to provide a stubborn defense against top and bottom, and to prevent a direct contact or dualism between throne and masses. The system turns with the bitterest hatred against the apostles of change in a bourgeoisie at that very time becoming conscious of its importance for the state; against the middle class which aims at emancipation from those above and wants to suppress those beneath and thus leads the way first to oligarchy and then to democracy; against the ideologists, the firebrands of Jacobinism, who without realizing it will bring about the tyranny of the masses; against the intellectual proletariat that wants to found the state on reason alone. In the eyes of the system the real people are not yet affected by this political arrogance; they only want the protection of the law for their persons, families, and property, the security of their daily bread, and low taxes. Once unleashed, the enormous physical force that resides in the masses leads to general collapse. For nations are like children or nervous women; they believe in ghosts, and there is no greater simpleton than the public. Hold the restless middle class in check with a firm hand, strengthen the conserving element of the aristocracy, keep the agitation away from the people, satisfy the economic wants of these broad strata, and then not stale theory but the natural principle of order will necessarily retain the upper hand.

Also rated as socially conservative are the professional orders. Examples: the quite Napoleonic practice (as we have already observed) of regarding the Christian religion and the Christian churches as conserving factors, especially the Catholic Church, which functions as the other great monarchical, hierarchically organized agency of indoctrination; again, the maintenance of state control over the denominations as associations requiring regulation, the insistence on peace between church and state, the antipathy to the Josephinian concept of a state church — in place of which the Metternich system aims at delimiting the competence of throne and altar and establishing an alliance between them. Church and state belong together, coordinated like body and soul, independent in their respective spheres of law, yet indivisible in the moral and social realm. These principles of ecclesiastical policy lack a specifically ethical and religious character; the supporting function of the church in the service of the principle of authority and preservation is what predominates, not meditation on the world to come. Entirely analogous to this is the high value placed on the military. But what is the attitude toward the bureaucracy? The system recognized very well the intimate interconnections between the external power-position of a state and its internal moral and material condition and allotted corresponding importance to the diplomatic and administrative apparatus; and yet, bureaucracy suffered here a condemnation as sharp as that meted out by Bismarck.It is the opposition of the political leadership-type to "half-cracked formalism," the antipathy of the conservative to bureaucratic liberalism, of authority to the fondness of officialdom for expedience.

Proteuslike, now as a religious or spiritual movement, now as a political movement, as mysticism and philanthropy, as liberalism and nationalism—in all these guises there is always concealed the destructure principle, the Revolution, Jacobinism. The honest revolutionaries are always the radicals. "I would have preferred Robespierre to the Abbé de Pradt!" The system, ever logical, standing on the either/or, the system, which admitted to preferring the open enemy to the hidden one every time and welcomed every danger as soon as it became tangible, accorded to the radicals a logic and consistency and hence a greater strength than liberalism had. Since Metternich's eyes were closed to the ethical content of the older liberalism, he was capable of seeing in it only verbiage, ideology, and dishonesty. But he foresaw that it is the liberals who make breaches through which the radicals penetrate into the fortress. They are the pacemakers of democracy; they are the pretenders while radicalism is the real thing; and the succeeding stages fall inexorably into line: the undermining of the monarchical system, the rule of liberalism, then of radicalism, anarchy, military despotism—or else there is chaos, "the unadulterated nothing." By rule of logic, popular sovereignty leads to communism, to the abolition of property, and the slaughter of its possessors. *Principiis obsta et respice finem!* Once a stone falls unnaturally out of the structure of the legal and social order as the century unwinds, the crumbling process will not be stopped short of the destruction of society. Even without a vision of what was inevitable in the dynamics of social development, the system clearly recognized that the tendency to politicize social life becomes the forerunner (ultimately pushed aside by the masses) of that other tendency to make the people as a homogeneous mass the sole possessor of the sovereign rights of the state with the right of social and economic self-determination; and it had a presentiment of the horrors the onset of which was to be experienced with trembling only by a later generation.

Under the heading of liberal-democratic movement and on a plane with the demand for equality, liberty, and constitution, the system likewise condemns "the shibboleth," the new notion of "nationality"; it traces it back, with some justification, to the great awakener, the Revolution, with its doctrine of unlimited rights for the people, and adds as its goal the dissolution of the established lawful social entities, that is, states of mixed nationality. In this survey we cannot go into the question of how the system dealt with the particular, directly threatening subproblem of the German and Italian desires for unity. Here we shall only touch on the general subject of the position taken by the "historic-organic" state of the system toward the great storm tide of the century that pressed on toward the formation of national states as a natural right of nations. The needs of the states stand higher than the claims of the nationalities. The nation is not recognized as a social body; there is no general right of the national cultures to the formation of ethnically unified states; there is no nation in the political sense, with individuality and a legal personality standing above the state; a right of national development exists only within the borders of existing states. Integral national states, to be sure, have the advantage of greater internal and external strength over states inhabited by a number of nations or different branches of one and the same people, but a higher right of existence is not immanent in them. In a real sense, the term nation is not suited to every people. The criterion for this is not a common language, descent, domicile, or spiritual life, but is taken, in individual cases, from history, which is understood as the product of the immutable physical character of the land and the psychological makeup of the people. Only those peoples whose various branches have demonstrated in history the will and the strength to overcome divisive forces in favor of political unity truly deserve the name nation and have the right to preserve their political cohesion. The deliberate unification of the segments of a people naturally and historically divided can only lead to artificial structures incapable of life. Rationalistic historicism and the social momentum of mankind collaborate with concrete interests of state, as one can see, using the right of the state to break up the right of nations.

The heterogenous nature of the social structure of political Europe and her individual states categorically requires the realization of this principle: unity in multiplicity. As a counterweight to disintegration or an unnatural striving for unity only the principle of federalism can adequately meet this need. Corresponding to it there is the union of the states into the *Corps social Europa* for the preservation of the external and internal equilibrium; corresponding to it, in smaller compass, are the German league of states and the Swiss Confederation; the never-realized *Lega Italica* would have fitted in with it; to it, finally, more or less every composite state has to conform by virtue of the decentralization of its parts and respect for the "diversity and peculiarity of language, mores, and habits, of climate and inherited nationality" so long as a strong crown holds things together. The first impulse for this federalistic idea of Metternich's, which differed sharply from the usual monolithic system of absolutism and centralism, may have come from the opposition of unitarism and federalism, which had divided the Mountain and the Girondins; doubtless the fissures in the German people and the character of the Austrian state were also substantial empirical sources of ideas.

Along with this supremely important principle of organization required in the struggle against chaos and destruction, what is also indispensable is forceful rule by the legally constituted authorities. Between the sphere of government and the sphere of the governed lies that of administration, which is to be sharply separated from the government. In demanding that the government must rule, not merely administer, the system made frequent reference to the Napoleonic model and, though following the federative principle in contrast to Napoleon's centralized administration, it always emphasized that governing must take place in the center, administration in the parts. The unity of the top leadership in the state should be provided in the government by a council of department heads under a premier who presides but does not take power into his own hands: thus the leadership of the state should be collegiate in operation with the ministers collectively responsible to the monarch, and the function of the already mentioned council of state should be merely a moral one.

Preservation is only possible with an active government, not one that abandons itself to "letting things go." With this we come to the new cardinal point, the question of whether to make preventive or repressive the measures which the system requires of the government in the midst of the raging social struggle; its duty is not repression, as Sybel,[13] for example, still thought, but prevention, "shrewdly foreseeing things"; but if one must act repressively, the punishment should at the same time have a preventive effect — a noteworthy analogy to Robert von

---

[13] Heinrich von Sybel, German historian. — Ed.

Mohl's[14] attempt to make preventive justice a separate branch of jurisprudence and to show how the state can prevent disruptions of the security of persons and property and restore law and order as quickly and completely as possible.

This preventive procedure and the confinement of repression to a secondary role, according to Metternich's system, has to be used above all against the three most dangerous instruments of the never-resting revolution: following Napoleon's example, against the secret societies, whether they be called Illuminati, Tugenbund, Burschenschaften, Carbonari, or whatever, or borrow the look of scientific or public-service purpose; next, against the specifically German menace of the universities, of the unscholarly, politically oriented teachers in the universities who follow after national and liberal phantoms, and of the students insofar as they are infected with this evil; finally, against the press as a poisoner and seducer of public opinion. The press leads the respectable German bourgeoisie astray and seeks to drive the world forward in a sort of steeplechase to God knows where. In itself not to be counted among the destructive forces, in itself valuable for human society, the press, under the cloak of freedom and impartiality, exercises the most arrant despotism, often springing from nothing but financial speculation. It can never be subjected to the regulation which it, like all other powers, needs, by Draconian punishment, but only by preventive censorship.

There still remains one final problem, which leads us back to the question of stability versus progress. How can a state leadership which is bound to such a rigid system still satisfy the needs of the advancing times? Perpetual standstill is of course just as contrary to nature as is fitful movement. The answer is logically unavoidable. Without letting itself be led astray by the slogan "spirit of the times," the government must carry out, at the right time, necessary legislative and administrative reforms; it should, however, make no concessions in regard to the eternal principles, may not dip into the capital of pure monarchy for the benefit of popular sovereignty, and may not arbitrarily change anything in the lawful status of social and legal institutions. Perhaps, however, it might take up carefully considered changes in the positive law. Rigid in the eternal principles, adaptable in regard to transitory statutes, ordinances, and regulations, the statesman should be firm and flexible at the same time—no doctrinaire, no ramrod, but a steel spring which bends under pressure yet withstands it and after relaxation of the pressure again returns to its earlier position. Politics is flexible; its limits are fixed principles. There is nothing more dangerous than allowing concessions to be wrung by force. Least of all are times of mass movement and critical social conditions suited to making concessions. In such times, standing still and steady is what is called for. The statesman must of course reckon with the strength of the things that can force him to submit; necessity can force him to suffer violations of the principles of law and order; in that case, however, he must at least see to providing legal sanction for changes that are in themselves illegal. Here the system has found the way to the realistic political insight of the genuine statesman: the true politician must take things as they are, and without illusions and complaints about what has happened he must adapt himself to the general situation, which he cannot help, hold fast to violated principles, and

---

[14] Nineteenth-century moderate liberal political scientist in Baden.—Ed.

save from shipwreck what can be saved. Often the dispassionate, tough-minded, and conscientious statesman must wait patiently to see how things develop, if it is impossible to go over immediately to the attack. Man, so this description of the ideal leader shows, cannot in the end, of course, anticipate the great decisions of the unseen powers; only in a precautionary and supporting role can he help nature along. Constitutions burn themselves out and lead to absurdity; revolutions collapse of their own weight; radicalism, having attained power, either destroys the world order or must be destroyed. If chaos occurs, then even this is only a phase in the eternal cycle of society, which does not die but changes and returns, often by very long routes, to the place where it started. The individual man is nothing against the forces of nature. He cannot create; he can only go along with the natural sequence of phenomena, help reject bad elements and further the development of the good. To endure to the end, however, is his duty: *si fractus illabatur orbis, impavidam ferient ruinae* —that is the keystone of the system of the archconservative social-philosopher and statesman; his own life remained true to his doctrine of the struggle against the destructive principle.

This is not the place to draw conclusions about present-day politics from our expositions. Even the purely historical critique of the Metternichian system must be brief within this space: there dwells within it no strong and living active principle. Without a more meaningful correlation to the idea of development, the idea of conservation could not satisfy the fullness of life. The belief in the perpetual struggle of two great forces and the disbelief in human creative power; the rejection of any middle line in the field of principles and the axiom that in troubled times large-scale reforms should not be carried out; the lumping together of all the major movements, from the Reformation up to "Prussianism" and "Teutonism" and the bourgeois and labor movements of the nineteenth century, in the concept of destructive revolution—all this led to a radicalism of one-sidedness which in practice often turned out to provide stability against active forces entitled to life in their time and was often unable to distinguish the positive in new things from the really destructive. But should we therefore deny to the intellectual content of this system any objective importance? Even if we do not speak further of the astounding vision which confronts us in some of the doctrines, this system can properly lay claim to being a European one comprehending the whole of society. It is a universal doctrine appropriate to the view that the new century and its social dynamic were the enemies; it is a principal heir of the supranational universalism of the prerevolutionary era; and it is the classic expression of archconservative thought in the period of the Restoration; it is a *credo* which may always claim its place in the history of political and social ideas, in the grandiose struggle of spiritual forces in recent history.

KARL GROOS (1861–1946), a lecturer in psychology and philosophy at the universities of Giessen and Tübingen, was especially interested in the psychological significance of games. His studies of Bismarck and Metternich offer pioneering examples of what today would be called psychohistory. In his book on Metternich, which he called "a study in the psychology of vanity," he directs his interest less to the content of Metternich's principles than to the inordinate pride the minister took in them. Without altogether denying Metternich's sincerity, Groos concludes in this extract that his obsession with principles reflected an inner need to rule and to identify with eternity.*

Karl Groos

Vain Neurotic

The Vain Man of Principle   Can Metternich be called a man of principle? In any case, the term must be clarified. In this regard one could first imagine a character free from any impulse to vanity who with quiet simplicity conducts himself in word and deed according to fixed maxims. Such a man would have nothing to do with our topic. What we mean, of course, is a personality who prides himself on constantly acting according to fixed principles and who is given to extolling this fidelity to principle ahead of everything else. Metternich did this in conversation and in writing with a lack of inhibition which must have been intolerable to his acquaintances if they took it without a sense of humor. The pedantic manner which people criticized in him and the impression of lofty serenity, which he himself sought to convey, are closely connected with this trait. When Talleyrand asked him in 1808 whether he had reflected on a conversation of the previous day and inquired how he now viewed the question under discussion (the partition of Turkey), Metternich replied grandly, "My principles do not change from one day to the next." "I am the least stubborn man," he wrote in 1822, "but the most persistent; nothing can make me deviate from my principles, so I am quite a difficult minister for my opponents." "The only ambition I am capable of," he

*From Karl Groos, *Fürst Metternich, Eine Studie zur Psychologie der Eitelkeit* (Stuttgart and Berlin: J. G. Cotta'sche Buchhandlung Nachfolger, 1922), pp. 47–63, omitting the original footnotes and source references. Translated by Keith Mostofi and Enno E. Kraehe.

assured Countess Lieven,[1] "is doing good." He claimed over and over again that he had always lived for duty, never for himself. As he puts it in his autobiographical memoir, "the role which we personally had to play in the events of our time fell to us not by our own choice, but was imposed solely by a sense of duty. Free of every ambition save that of measuring up, in good conscience, to the tasks which a combination of unparalleled circumstances had heaped upon our head at the start of our ministry, we have never strayed from the path which seemed marked out for us by simple justice." If because of this he regarded himself wholly as a martyr to duty, he found his only consolation in the consciousness of the services he rendered daily to the "triumph of principles."

It is not without amusement that one sees how Metternich chose to defend himself when he was forced on one occasion to act all too flagrantly against those high principles in which he beheld not merely a system but "a world order." When he recognized, on assuming the ministry, that the state, after Napoleon's victories, was to be rescued only by "adaptation" to the hated "French system," he wrote to Emperor Francis, "My principles are unchangeable, but there is no arguing with necessity. . . . We must therefore, from the day of peace on, confine our policy exclusively to tacking, to evading, to flattering." In his later life the Prince would scarcely have expressed himself so openly even to his confidants.

Principles as Mask That, however, suggests another question. It could be that Metternich's protestation of loyalty to principles did not in any way spring from vanity, but only revealed the mask of the hypocritical man who in his inner being ridicules the maxims he feigns and is entirely conscious of acting from other motives: perhaps out of strictly realistic concern for the fatherland, but perhaps, too, from more unworthy impulses arising from egoism. The political as well as the moral propositions constantly on the lips of such a man would then in the final analysis be nothing more than means of deception, intended to mask conscious ambition, the greed for power, selfishness, and the desire for enjoyment. I do not know whether one encounters this simple sketch of a stage villain with unusual frequency in the intricate reality of the psyche in which "bovarysm"[2] plays such a great role. Be that as it may, insofar as it is a question of principles, it cannot be applied to Metternich. Naturally it cannot be denied that the crafty diplomat also used his principles as weapons the better to resist an opponent. But just as Treitschke,[3] despite his indignation at Metternich's "mendacious self-praise" and the "deep insincerity of his spirit," still concedes that the State Chancellor never doubted the excellence of the system he championed, so one could even say more generally that he not only took the principles he advocated seriously, as something sacred, but that he was also convinced that he was guided by them in his actions. He boasted of this in innumerable cases where the intention of cheating an opponent was completely absent. His self-image was certainly much nobler, purer, and grander than his real ego; but in his colossal smugness he rarely made this distinction very clear to himself, and under its influence whenever he reflected

---

[1] Countess Dorothea Lieven, wife of the Russian ambassador in London and intimate friend of Metternich. — Ed.

[2] A romantic conception of oneself, after Gustave Flaubert's *Madame Bovary.* — Ed.

[3] German historian. See below, p. 73. — Ed.

about his nature, he would be entirely deaf to the voices of any egotistical motives that might possibly have been concealed behind the high principles. We shall come back to this point.

Repose and Order Nothing has yet been said about the content of the principles Metternich followed as a statesman. It is well-known that they can be most succinctly expressed by the words he himself used again and again: "repose and order." As the sign of political health, peace is the goal to which he devoted himself in the struggle with the forces breeding disorder and sickness, which in the broadest sense of the word are to be described as "revolutionary"; for Metternich, Luther's Reformation and Napoleon's assaults on the peace of Europe were as much manifestations of the revolutionary spirit as was the demand of the liberals for a parliament. Order is the form necessary to realization of the goal. "Health and equilibrium are identical concepts, like the concepts of repose and order, without which peace is not possible." To order belong the institutions, preserved for thousands of years, which make it possible for nations to have internal peace and therewith the only freedom that Metternich recognized. These institutions are, above all, the "old" monarchy, not limited by a liberal constitution, and the authority of the church going hand in hand with it. The great masses would fall into chaos if they were not cared for from above. The "sovereign" people is the same as "an incompetent who needs a guardian."

If one considers the era in which the aristocrat Metternich lived, his devotion to the preservation of an absolute monarchy supported by the church is thoroughly understandable. "I learned," he says in his autobiographical memoir "to judge how hard it is to erect a society on

new foundations if the old are destroyed." The belief in the old order, however, is more than understandable; it appears as a necessary consequence of circumstances the moment one focuses on the fact that the direction of the Austrian state happened to be entrusted to this man during the great storms of his epoch. As even Treitschke acknowledges, "by astutely holding back and then at the right moment throwing in the resources of the state," Metternich succeeded in bringing Austrian power after the Wars of Liberation to a marvelous fullness which recalled the days of Wallenstein. "Once this goal was attained, if the state, composed as it was of so many nationalities, was to maintain itself on the conquered heights, it had to be based on dynastic interests and, with guarded distrust, stand opposed to the demand of the nationalities for unity and freedom. Metternich realized rightly that his Austria was a power dependent on perseverance."

Here is the basis for explaining how the self-esteem of this man, inclined by nature to vanity, soared to an almost pathological "immeasurable arrogance," so naïvely expressed as to be otherwise almost incomprehensible in one of his undeniable sagacity. He felt himself to be, and was also considered by his admirers to be, the man of destiny chosen "to strike down the German Revolution" as he had "defeated the conqueror of the world." For ten years, he wrote the Countess Lieven in 1819, he had not ceased asking himself why fate had chosen him alone from millions of men "to be continually face to face with Napoleon." He is the heavy boundary marker or guardstone which immovably keeps its place "to stop those who go too fast and on the wrong side." He saw himself as the "rock of order" called to withstand the flood of revolution. In this conviction he died. Shortly before his death, Alexander von Hübner[4] visited him. In farewell, the old man said repeatedly and with emphasis, "I was a rock of order." "I had already closed the doors behind me," Hübner reported, "when I gently opened them again in order to view the great statesman once more. There he sat at his writing desk, pen in hand, his gaze pensively directed upward, in an erect posture, cold, proud, aristocratic, as I had seen him so often in the state chancellery in the full splendor of power. The foreshadowings of death, which I thought I noticed in his last days, had retreated from his countenance. A ray of sunlight brightened the room, and the reflected light illuminated his noble features. After some time he noticed me at the doorway, fixed a look of sincere benevolence upon me for a long time, then turned away and said to himself half-aloud: 'a rock of order.'"

Politics of Principle Perhaps it is appropriate here to follow with a general observation on the politics of principle. If it is true that statesmen make their decisions deductively, so to speak, from definitely formulated principles that are said to serve them as guidelines, the fact is by no means self-evident. Radicalism, if it is not merely negative, will certainly be driven to such a method, because, in order to erect a wholly new structure, it is in need of ideals. On the other hand, a politician who does not think of overthrowing the old forms of political life will always be well able to make decisions from case to case according to circumstances simply by asking himself what best serves the power position of his state. For this, the formulation of special axioms is hardly necessary, because the claims of power are "always self-evident,"

to paraphrase an expression of F. T. Vischer.[5] I would like to assume that this describes the natural method of the "unphilosophical" statesman; others will charge him (as happened even with Bismarck, by the way) with a lack of ideas, while he in turn is given to labeling their principles as ideology out of touch with this world. Now if even a conservative-minded politician senses the need to acknowledge general maxims, this need can spring from an inner compulsion to rationalize one's actions; it can, however, likewise be stimulated externally by revolutionary aspirations rising up in the people and forcing the responsible statesman to conceptualize his own viewpoint. With Metternich, not only the second, but also the first, motive was operative, since he was partial to general formulations—or, as he himself put it, "formulas." Both motives were sustained by the heightened self-esteem that commonly permeates the conscious man of principle and which in the case of Metternich's contemporaries, Emperor Nicholas of Russia and his predecessor Alexander, also accompanied the "politics of principle." Schiemann[6] said of the latter, "What he did had to be cloaked in the mantel of noble principle, even where questions of power and interest were decisive."

Maxims and Predispositions We define maxims—as should already be evident from the foregoing—as the conscious principles of actions; predispositions (the expression is chosen with Kant's ethics in mind), as the drives, springing from innate instincts and acquired habits, which in contrast to the former are irrational in their immediate nature. Both

---

[4] Austrian ambassador to Paris at the time (1859). —Ed.

[5] Friedrich Theodor Vischer (1807–1887), German philosopher and satirical writer.—Ed.

[6] Theodor Schiemann, German historian of Russia.—Ed.

these forces, as everyone knows, are frequently in conflict with one another; they can, however, also go hand in hand, as is the case with the "harmonious soul" or—to take a more familiar example—with a man who in public life devotes himself to definite political ideas and in doing so satisfies his ambition at the same time. With that we come up against a fact, to which the discussion of principles used only as a mask has led us: Even in the convinced man of principle there is an unintentional veiling of his innermost being, which is connected with his stress on general principles.

In my studies of Bismarck, I frequently started with instincts, especially that of inborn combativeness, in order to make his individuality clear in my mind. . . . As I expressly emphasized, I used this approach, which probably appears all too "zoological" to the votaries of this great man, with deliberate one-sidedness as an experiment to see how one could work with it. That the method chosen offers certain advantages in dealing with a man like Bismarck, in whom historians too have stressed "the unbroken strength of his instincts," seems to me to be proven. With Metternich, the situation is somewhat different. To be sure, he would not have been an active man if his drives and predispositions had not influenced his actions. But in his self-portrayal they are much more heavily veiled by the strong emphasis on the principles guiding him than is the case with Bismarck's blunt genius. Precisely for that reason it is not unimportant to refer to the occasional remarks which disclose the undercurrent arising from the deeper strata of the innate individuality and bearing with it the maxims visible on the surface. In doing this I will confine myself to the concepts of repose and order.

First, concerning the principle of order,

we have seen that for Metternich it is best ensured in the absolute monarchy. The conviction that he must in this sense be a rock of order he justified as the *theoretical* result of his reflection on the laws prevalent in history. For here it is a question of an axiom that in his view has held good since most ancient times; one is not supposed to discover new principles, he says in one place, but should be satisfied with those "which have governed human society for four thousand years." So much for the maxims of reason which induced him to fight for the preservation of the old monarchical system. If we now ask about the motive impulses that stand behind the ratiocinations, we will be referred to the fact that without a doubt there existed in Metternich an innate need to rule and that in Austria, as the responsible statesman, he could best satisfy this need by preserving the existing political order. He was, as Strobl von Ravelsberg[7] says, "the essence of a born ruler." The will to power of a directing type of person will, in the situation in which Metternich found himself, aim not at overthrowing but at preserving the existing order, so long as it offers him a favorable opportunity for action. Thus maxim and predisposition operate in the same direction.

To be sure, this tendency, stemming from the realm of instinct, hardly ever finds direct expression in the Prince's portrayal of himself, but it glimmers through clearly enough in some of his utterances. The wearer of the crown basically does not impress him very much. "If you knew," he writes Countess Lieven, "what I think of the dwellers in the highest regions, you would right away take me for a Jacobin." At best, the emperors and kings know too little of the real world

---

[7] Author of a biography of Metternich published in 1906–1907.—Ed.

to rule it with success; if he himself were a radical or demagogue, it would not be hard for him "to cast down the mightiest of the earth." But as minister he finds himself in a position such as his will to power requires. And so outwardly, of course, he gives in, like a mere servant, or "helper," of his Emperor Francis; but he well knows that he controls the monarch and thus holds absolute power in his hands — of course, only to use it as the emperor intends. "The emperor always does what I want, but, likewise, I always want only what he should do." Another position in the monarchy could not have satisfied him, because all half measures, as he often emphasized, were repugnant to him, and "playing a secondary role" was not in keeping with the "independence" of his character. Therefore his self-esteem tells him that he and only he is the man qualified to lead, while no one else will do. "For that reason, I consider myself stronger than most of my contemporaries." As a trait characteristic of the vain directing type, let us also cite the passage from a letter to Countess Lieven of January 5, 1819, in which Metternich recounts how the apparently very excitable English ambassador to Vienna, Lord Charles Stewart, took leave of him. After passionate embraces, Stewart finally kissed Metternich's hand; of this the Prince writes, "and I have never told him that I liked having my hand kissed."

That a predisposition grounded in Metternich's nature also corresponds to the principle of repose, Treitschke has expressed with the phrase he occasionally used: "blissful repose." In the differentiation of men into various types, the distinction between those who are constantly *rerum novarum* (and *novarum commotionum*) *cupidi*,[8] and those to whom peace and perseverance seem much more appropriate, will be present. If Metternich, in countless reiterations, celebrates *le repos* as "the first of all boons for the entire human society," at first one can only deduce from this his political conviction that the progress he despises disturbs "the world's sleep," as Hebbel[9] puts it, and would plunge nations into misery. But he has also frequently emphasized that it is his inner nature that resists change and unrest. Thus he wrote in 1819 from his estate at Konigswart, where the peace and calm reigning there produced in him a mood of contentment, "I am not one of those who think that movement is the purpose of life." In a letter from the year 1827 he affirms that he had a "need of invincible repose"; that was the secret of his heart. From Leghorn he addressed to Countess Lieven the words, "I have left Florence with the regret that comes naturally to me on leaving a familiar place — a very comprehensible feeling if the place is agreeable, pure instinct if it is not. I believe I have already told you . . . that I can never leave even the meanest inn without a certain twinge of regret. If I were a horse, I would adore my stable and my rack." Unrest offended him, and he had a deeply rooted antipathy against its authors: "God has . . . given me a calm disposition, and fate has put me in the whirlpool." There is something in his nature, as he emphasizes another time, that bristles up at men who carry in themselves an impulse to unrest: "adventurers" like Pozzo or Capodistria, but, in somewhat different form, also "at the likes of Chateaubriand, Canning, Haugwitz, Stein, and so forth."

The predisposition and temper running parallel to the maxims, however, are still not exhaustively comprehended

---

[8] The phrase means "desirous of new things (and new commotion)." — Ed.

[9] Christian Friedrich Hebbel (1813–1863), German dramatist. — Ed.

in the expression, "blissful repose," as used by Treitschke. Metternich loved all that is enduring in the world and he felt himself to be a power of steadfastness, because repose—"this calm which alone bestows real strength"—produces the impression of greatness and stateliness. Thus even this aspect of his nature becomes involved with his heightened self-esteem. If he liked to speak of the "calm innate in him," he meant by this not blissful repose but the imperviousness of his being to change. In the year 1819 he wrote to his daughter Marie from Teplitz, where six years before he had signed the Holy Alliance, "Everything has changed since then, except me." He boasts of always going his own straight way without turning his head; the others who are not capable of this must of necessity sometimes go with him, sometimes cross his path. "I have the conviction," one reads in a note to Countess Lieven, "of never having retreated from my position: the first moral element in me is immobility." Even the mausoleum he wished to erect for himself and his family in the Egyptian style, like no other in Bohemia or perhaps in Europe, was meant to proclaim the grandeur of permanence. "I love everything," he adds, "that defies time." A solid bridge, which he built at Königswart, was supposed to look as if it "originated with the world." Thus, it was to be a symbolic expression of his being: "I have had a column erected there whose inscription will say that I ("I" is underscored in the letter) built the bridge." The rulers of ancient Egypt must have felt this way toward their more imposing buildings.

HENRY A. KISSINGER (b. 1923), German born and American educated, is a professor of government and member of the Center for International Affairs at Harvard University. He has held several posts with the federal government, most recently that of foreign-policy adviser to the President. Although trained as a political scientist and best known for his writing on nuclear strategy, Kissinger has also been interested in applying his precepts to history. Thus his book on Metternich and Castlereagh, while lacking the historian's mastery of the sources, is rich in insights and provocative generalizations about "the nature of statesmanship"— to quote the title of the chapter from which this selection is taken.*

Henry A. Kissinger

Responsible Statesman
of International Order

Few periods present such a dramatic contrast of personalities or illustrate so well problems of organizing a legitimate order as the interval between the defeat of Napoleon in Russia and the Congress of Verona. While Napoleon dominated Europe, policy based on a conception of national strategy was impossible. The fate of states depended on the will of the conqueror, and safety could be found only in adaptation to the French system. But Napoleon's defeat in Russia made clear that Europe could no longer be governed by force, that the man of will would have to find safety in a recognition of limits. And the disintegration of the Grande Armée obliged the European nations to define anew their place in the international order, to create a balance of forces to discourage future aggression, and to wrest out of the chaos of the disintegrated structure of the eighteenth century some principle of organization which would ensure stability. . . .

While the conqueror attempts to equate his will with the structure of obligations and the prophet seeks to dissolve organization in a moment of transcendence, the statesman strives to keep latent the tension between organization and inspiration; to create a pattern of obligations sufficiently spontaneous to reduce to a minimum the necessity for the application of force, but, at the same time, of

*From Henry A. Kissinger, *A World Restored: Metternich, Castlereagh and the Problems of Peace 1812-1822* (Boston: Houghton Mifflin Company, 1957), pp. 315–316, 317–324, omitting the original footnotes. Reprinted by permission of the publisher, Houghton Mifflin Company.

sufficient firmness not to require the legitimization of a moment of exaltation. It is not surprising that Castlereagh and Metternich were statesmen of the equilibrium, seeking security in a balance of forces. Their goal was stability, not perfection, and the balance of power is the classic expression of the lesson of history that no order is safe without physical safeguards against aggression. Thus the new international order came to be created with a sufficient awareness of the connection between power and morality; between security and legitimacy. No attempt was made to found it entirely on submission to a legitimizing principle; this is the quest of the prophet and dangerous because it presupposes the self-restraint of sanctity. But neither was power considered self-limiting; the experience of the conqueror had proved the opposite. Rather, there was created a balance of forces which, because it conferred a relative security, came to be generally accepted, and whose relationships grew increasingly spontaneous as its legitimacy came to be taken for granted.

To be sure, the international order had been founded on a misunderstanding and a misconception; a misunderstanding because the conference system which Castlereagh created as a symbol of harmony was used by Metternich as a diplomatic weapon to isolate his opponents. And a misconception because Castlereagh equated stability with a *consciousness* of reconciliation. But the belief that all threats, not only those of universal dominion, would be interpreted in the same manner by every power proved a tragic mistake. It is the essence of a revolutionary period that the attack on the "legitimate" order obliterates all differences within it; but by the same token it is the nature of a stable period that the acceptance of its legitimacy makes it safe to con-

test on local or peripheral issues. Because after Napoleon's overthrow the international order no longer contained a revolutionary power, no real motive for Britain's continued participation in the conference system existed, all the less so since the chief threat to the international order, the twin movements of liberalism and nationalism were not considered dangerous in Great Britain. Thus the conference system led either to a dispute on peripheral issues, which seemed petty and distasteful to Castlereagh, or it exhibited a unanimity over a threat that Britain could not admit as an international problem. When the unity of Europe came to pass, it was not because of the self-evidence of its necessity, as Castlereagh had imagined, but through a cynical use of the conference machinery to define a legitimizing principle of social repression; not through Castlereagh's good faith, but through Metternich's manipulation.

But even with these qualifications, it remains to be asked how it was possible to create an approximation to a European government, however tenuous, and with Britain as an observer on the sidelines. What enabled Metternich to emerge as the Prime Minister of Europe? It was Metternich's misfortune that history in the latter half of the nineteenth century was written by his opponents, to whom he was anathema both by principle and policy and who ascribed his achievements to a contradictory combination of cunning and good fortune, of mediocrity and incompetent adversaries, without explaining how such a man managed to place his stamp on his period. For the documents of his period leave no doubt that for over a generation nothing occurred in Europe which was not shaped by Metternich either directly or through his opposition. To be sure, Metternich was aided by the instability of the Tsar and the indecisiveness of the Prussian King. But the Tsar's mercurial temper might also have resulted in a new crusade; and although Alexander's instability was there for everyone to exploit, only Metternich managed to achieve a personal domination. On the other hand, Metternich's own interpretation of the superiority of his philosophical maxims is refuted by their conventionality, while mere deviousness could not have duped all of Europe for over a decade. Rather, Metternich's successes were due to two factors: that the unity of Europe was not Metternich's invention, but the common conviction of *all* statesmen; and because Metternich was the last diplomat of the great tradition of the eighteenth century, a "scientist" of politics, coolly and unemotionally arranging his combinations in an age increasingly conducting policy by "causes." The maxims on which he so prided himself had therefore a psychological, but not a philosophical, significance: because he was convinced, indeed cocksure, of his rectitude, he could soberly and cynically evaluate the maxims of others as forces to be exploited. Because he considered policy a science, he permitted no sentimental attachments to interfere with his measures. There was not found in Metternich's diplomacy the rigid dogmatism which characterized his choice of objectives nor the undisciplined sentimentality of Alexander's conduct. And because, despite his vanity, he was always ready to sacrifice the form of a settlement for the substance, his victories became, not wounds, but definitions of a continuing relationship.

Metternich was aided by an extraordinary ability to grasp the fundamentals of a situation and a profound psychological insight which enabled him to dominate his adversaries. In 1805, he was almost alone in pointing out that Prussia was no longer the state of Frederick the Great; in 1812, he was one of the first to realize the essential transformation brought about by Napoleon's defeat; after 1815, he understood better than anyone the nature of the social transformation preparing itself in Europe, and that he decided to defy the tide may be a reflection on his statesmanship but not on his insight. He therefore had the great advantage over his adversaries that he knew what he wanted; and if his goals were sterile, they were fixed. "Everybody wants something," wrote Metternich at the height of the Greek crisis, "without having any idea how to obtain it and the really intriguing aspect of the situation is that nobody quite knows how to achieve what he desires. But because I know what I want and what the others *are capable of* [Metternich's italics] I am completely prepared." That this statement was boastful, vain, and smug does not detract from its truth.

But all his diplomatic skill would have availed Metternich nothing, had he not operated in a framework in which his invocation of the unity of Europe could appear as something other than a euphemism for Austrian national interest. The early nineteenth century was a transition period, and, as in all such periods, the emergence of a new pattern of obligation for a time served only to throw into sharp relief the values being supplanted. The political structure of the eighteenth century had collapsed, but its ideals were still familiar. And because those ideals were derived from a rationalistic philosophy validated by its truth, they claimed a universal applicability. To Metternich's contemporaries the unity of Europe was a reality, the very ritualism of whose invocation testified to its hold on the general consciousness. Regional differences were recognized, but they were considered local variations of a greater whole. Unity was not yet equated with identity, nor the claims of the nation with the dictates of morality. All of Metternich's colleagues were therefore products of essentially the same culture, professing the same ideals, sharing similar tastes. They understood each other, not only because they could converse with facility in French, but because in a deeper sense they were conscious that the things they shared were much more fundamental than the issues separating them. When Metternich introduced the Italian opera in Vienna, or Alexander brought German philosophy to Russia, they were not being consciously tolerant or even aware that they were importing something "foreign." The ideal of "excellence" still was more important than that of origin. Thus the Russian Prime Minister, Capo d'Istria, was a Greek, the Russian ambassador in Paris, Pozzo di Borgo, was a Corsican, while Richelieu, the French Prime Minster, had been governor of Odessa. Wellington gave military advice to Austria in its campaign against Murat, and in 1815 both Prussia and Austria asked Stein to serve as their ambassador with the Assembly of the Confederation. And Metternich with his cosmopolitan education and rationalist philosophy, Austrian only by the accident of feudal relationships, could be imagined equally easily as the minister of any other state. If he had any special ties to Austria, they derived from a philosophical not a national identification, because the principles Austria represented were closest to his own maxims, because Austria, the polyglot Empire, was a macrocosm of his cosmopolitan values. "For a long time now," he wrote to Wellington in 1824, "Europe has had for me the quality of a fatherland [*patrie*]."

For these reasons, Metternich was effective not only because he was persuasive but, above all, because he was plausible.

Of all his colleagues he was best able to appeal to the maxims of the eighteenth century, partly because they corresponded to his own beliefs, but, more importantly, because Austria's interests were identical with those of European repose. And because the end-result of Metternich's policy was stability and Austria's gain was always intangible, his extraordinary cynicism, his cold-blooded exploitation of the beliefs of his adversaries did not lead to a disintegration of all restraint, as the same tactics were to do later in the hands of Bismarck. Metternich's policy was thus one of status quo *par excellence,* and conducted, not by marshalling a superior force, but by obtaining a voluntary submission to his version of legitimacy. Its achievement was a period of peace lasting for over a generation without armament races or even the threat of a major war. And when the change came after 1848, it could be integrated into the existing structure without leading to the disintegration of Austria or to permanent revolution.

But its failure was the reverse side of this success. The identification of stability with the status quo in the middle of a revolutionary period reinforced the tendency towards rigidity of Austria's domestic structure and led eventually to its petrifaction. The very dexterity of Metternich's diplomacy obscured the real nature of his achievements, that he was merely hiding the increasing anachronism of Austria in a century of nationalism and liberalism; that he was but delaying the inevitable day of reckoning. To be sure, a truly successful policy for a polyglot Empire may have been impossible in a century of nationalism. And the Emperor would certainly have opposed any serious effort of domestic reform with his characteristic obtuse stubbornness. Nevertheless, the end of the Napoleonic war marked the last moment for Austria to attempt to brave the coming storm by adaptation, to wrench itself loose from the past, however painful the process. But Metternich's marvellous diplomatic skill enabled Austria to avoid the hard choice between domestic reform and revolutionary struggle; to survive with an essentially unaltered domestic structure in a century of rationalized administration; to continue a multi-national Empire in a period of nationalism. So agile was Metternich's performance that it was forgotten that its basis was diplomatic skill and that it left the fundamental problems unsolved, that it was manipulation and not creation. For diplomacy can achieve a great deal through the proper evaluation of the factors of international relations and by their skillfull utilization. But it is not a substitute for conception; its achievements ultimately will depend on its objectives, which are defined outside the sphere of diplomacy and which diplomacy must treat as given. So resourceful was Metternich that for a time he could make a performance of juggling appear as the natural pattern of international relations; so dexterous were his combinations that during a decade they obscured the fact that what seemed the application of universal principles was in reality the *tour de force* of a solitary figure.

Only a shallow historicism would maintain that successful policies are always possible. There existed no easy solution for Austria's tragic dilemma; that it could adapt itself by giving up its soul or that it could defend its values and in the process bring about their petrifaction. Any real criticism of Metternich must therefore attack, not his ultimate failure, but his reaction to it. It is Metternich's smug self-satisfaction with an essentially technical virtuosity which prevented him from achieving the tragic stature he might

have, given the process in which he was involved. Lacking in Metternich is the attribute which has enabled the spirit to transcend an impasse at so many crises of history: the ability to contemplate an abyss, not with the detachment of a scientist, but as a challenge to overcome—or to perish in the process. Instead one finds a bitter-sweet resignation which was not without its own grandeur, but which doomed the statesman of the anachronistic Empire in his primary ambition: to become a symbol of conservatism for posterity. For men become myths, not by what they know, nor even by what they achieve, but by the tasks they set for themselves.

Metternich had learned the lessons of the eighteenth-century cabinet diplomacy too well. Its skilful sense of proportion was appropriate for a period whose structure was unchallenged and whose components were animated by a consciousness of their safety; but it was sterile in an era of constant flux. Whenever Metternich operated within a fixed framework, when an alliance had to be constructed or a settlement negotiated, his conduct was masterly. Whenever he was forced to create his own objectives, there was about him an aura of futility. Because he sought tranquillity in the manipulation of factors he treated as given, the statesman of repose became the prisoner of events. Because he never fought a battle he was not certain of winning, he failed in becoming a symbol. He understood the forces at work better than most of his contemporaries, but this knowledge proved of little avail, because he used it almost exclusively to deflect their inexorable march, instead of placing it into his service for a task of construction. Thus the last vestige of the eighteenth century had to prove the fallacy of one of the maxims of the Enlightenment, that knowledge was power.

And for this reason, too, the final result of Metternich's policies had the quality of a series of ironies: that the policy of the statesman who most prided himself on the universality of his maxims lost its flexibility with the death of one man; that its structure was disintegrated by Prussia, the power he had conceived as one of its pillars, and that its legitimacy collapsed through the efforts, not of a representative of the social revolution or the middle class, but of the most traditionalist segment of Prussian society: Otto von Bismarck, whose ancestry antedated even that of the Prussian monarchs and who nevertheless completed the work of the futile revolutions which Metternich had mastered.

The two statesmen of repose were therefore both defeated in the end by their domestic structure: Castlereagh by ignoring it, Metternich by being too conscious of its vulnerability. But their achievements remain, not only in the long period of peace they brought about, but also in their impact on their time. The concert of Europe which emerged out of the Napoleonic wars was almost identical with their notion of the equilibrium, and the conference system which maintained it was Castlereagh's personal creation. It was he who mediated the differences of the Coalition and who, throughout his life, remained the conscience of the Alliance, even after he was forced into an increasingly passive role. Almost singlehandedly, he identified British security with Continental stability; and while in time the realities of an insular mentality reasserted themselves, British participation had lasted long enough to launch the new order without catastrophe. And Metternich, however he might struggle against the term "Metternich system," summed up the meaning of a generation of struggle. Between 1809 and 1848, it was possible to disagree with him, to detest him, but never to escape him. He was the High Priest of the Holy Alliance, the recognized interpreter of its maxims. He was the manipulator of the conference system, where his opponents suddenly found themselves isolated through the dexterous utilization of their own proposals. The very bitterness of the attacks on him testified to his central role. Anonymously, obliquely, indirectly, he demonstrated that policy may be based on knowledge, but that its conduct is an art.

PAUL W. SCHROEDER (b. 1927) is an American scholar now a professor at the University of Illinois. Although he won the Beveridge prize of the American Historical Association for a work on American-Japanese relations, his main interest has been Austrian diplomacy. He independently explored the archives in Vienna and reached conclusions considerably less flattering to Metternich than those of Srbik and Kissinger—although he modestly reminds us that his judgments pertain to a relatively short period. The following excerpt is taken from his book dealing with the congresses of Troppau, Laibach, and Verona.*

Paul W. Schroeder

Short-range Opportunist

Before attempting to add my bit to the acrid and not wholly edifying controversy over Metternich, I wish to stress two points by way of precaution. First, my own interpretation covers only Metternich's foreign policy during 1820–1823, and is thus at most a limited contribution to a general interpretation of Metternich's policy. This condition applies to all the rest of this chapter, even where it is not explicitly stated. Second, the evaluation of Metternich's policy given here is intended to be simply descriptive and historical, not moral. Even where I use words unavoidably charged with moral connotations (e.g., "repressive," "standstill") in characterizing Metternich's policy,

the intent is to give an accurate description, not a moral judgment.

Plainly, it would be presumptuous as well as futile for me to attempt in a brief space a point-by-point analysis and critique of Srbik's interpretation of Metternich. Srbik's main thesis, however, has become familiar and widely accepted, and has influenced to a greater or lesser extent such historians as Hugo Hantsch, Werner Näf, Constantin de Grunwald, Hans Rieben, and, most recently, Henry A. Kissinger. According to this interpretation, Metternich was a man of many faults and shortcomings, indeed, but withal a political figure far removed from the blind reactionary pictured by nineteenth-

*From Paul W. Schroeder, *Metternich's Diplomacy at Its Zenith, 1820–1823* (Austin: University of Texas Press, 1962), pp. 240–244, 249–266, omitting most of the original footnotes. By permission of University of Texas Press and Paul W. Schroeder.

century historians. Despite grave mistakes, he was, all in all, a constructive European statesman. His program for Austria and Europe was based on a system of coherent principles, not a patchwork of day-to-day diplomatic maneuvers; his policy was highly conservative, but definitely not reactionary.

The objection to this construction of Metternich, in my opinion, is that, though persuasive and convincing at first appearance, it does not, when applied to the period under consideration, seem to fit the evidence at hand. My own impression, in dealing with Metternich from 1820 to 1823, is that, instead of finding the long-range principles and plans of a constructive European statesman, one is continually confronted in the documents with the short-range maneuvers and expedients of a repressive Austrian diplomat. Three basic questions regarding Metternich's policy and attitudes in this period may explain and defend this conclusion. First, was his policy constructive? Second, was it "European"? Third, was it genuinely conservative? The answer to each question, properly understood and qualified, must, I believe, be in the negative.

As to the first, Metternich's policy in this period was not constructive for the simple reason that he was not trying to construct anything. His aim was not to make things happen, but to prevent things from happening; not to meet problems in some positive way, but simply to restrain and prevent political action, change, innovation, and movement of all kinds. In Germany his aim was to hold down political movement by so organizing and directing the Confederation as to make such movement impossible, or nearly so. In Italy his goal was so to crush the Italian revolutions as to leave no spark which might set off future change and agitation, and to reorganize the Ital-

ian governments, strengthen the Austrian hegemony, and place the Italian states under great-power supervision—all in order to prevent change and movement. In the Russo-Turk crisis all his diplomatic activity was designed to prevent Russia from going to war because it opened up all sorts of possibilities for change and movement in Europe. With France and the Spanish revolution, again, his whole policy was designed to prevent French intervention if possible and to limit and control it if it could not be prevented, because it was vital to keep a restless nation like France from undertaking an active policy at home or abroad.

The same abhorrence of change governed Metternich's attitude and policy toward all the great powers. Prussia was for Austria a menace and a rival so long as she entertained plans for a constitution. Once persuaded by Metternich that she should make no change at all in her fundamental institutions, Prussia was accepted as a safe and loyal ally. Before 1820 Metternich feared Russia more than any other state, because she was a source of political movement and change; after 1820 the Tsarist government was Austria's strongest support, because Metternich had, as he liked to say, steered Alexander and Russia out of their vagaries and onto a fixed (unchanging) course. France was inherently changeable, and therefore inherently dangerous. So long as British policy remained thoroughly conservative at home and abroad, Metternich could accept everything about Great Britain—her constitution, her parliamentary system, even her civil liberties. Once, however, England adopted a policy of accepting and even encouraging political change, Metternich quickly discovered that the English government was based on thoroughly bad principles, and that her constitution, her parliamentary system, and her civil liberties were nothing but highroads toward the revolution in which England was doomed to disintegrate.

This tendency to deplore and restrain all political movement, evident not only in Metternich's major decisions and actions, but also in numerous lesser ones, is so strong that it tempts one to the sweeping assertion that Metternich had no real foreign-policy goal in these years other than to prevent change. Every other goal which can legitimately be ascribed to him—preventing war, preserving the alliance, crushing revolutions, and "reforming" and strengthening governments— can be understood correctly, insofar as he actually pursued these goals, as a part of this general policy.

To argue, as I have, that Metternich's policy was one of repression and standstillism is not to imply that everything he did was wrong. His actions in the Russo-Turk crisis or the French-Spanish imbroglio, for example, might well be justified as the defense of a *status quo* which was better than any practicable change. It is quite arguable that Austria's internal weaknesses, together with the personality of her Emperor, made a policy of standstillism the only one possible. The only point here is that it is hard to see how such a purely negative policy can be labeled "constructive."

A further obstacle to such a label is the sheer inadequacy of the programs Metternich recommended to meet the fundamental problems of state in such areas as Naples, the rest of Italy, or Spain. Here a striking contrast between Metternich as diplomat and as statesman becomes evident. As a diplomat, Metternich possessed almost all the requisite talents. He was perceptive in his appraisal of the relevant factors in each situation, keenly analytical of his own and his opponent's positions, fertile in expedients, and readily adapt-

able to changed situations. His dealings with Alexander, Capodistrias, and Tatistchev demonstrate these abilities particularly well, but other examples could also be cited. Yet when Metternich came to devising programs and policies of government, these qualities of realism, farsightedness, flexibility, and skillful articulation of means to ends apparently abandoned him. . . .

One need not judge Metternich by modern standards of the welfare state to arrive at an unfavorable verdict on his approach to fundamental problems of state. He lagged behind the better standards of his own time. His own emissaries—De Menz, Daiser, and Brunetti[1] —showed insights and programs better than his. If enlightened despotism, as has been said, was the deathbed repentance of absolute monarchy, Metternich, in this period at least, never repented. He showed no great zeal for the aims of enlightened despotism—the promotion of industry and agriculture, the advancement of education and learning, the elevation of the physical lot of the worker and the peasant, and the development of the resources of the state—while he repudiated its fundamental premise—that the state and its monarch exist to promote the welfare of its subjects—as part of the false philosophy and philanthropy of the eighteenth century.

It may be objected that this appraisal leaves out Metternich's most important contribution to statecraft, his contribution to the maintenance of European peace and order. His most vital insight was the recognition that liberalism and nationalism, left unchecked, would lead to the wars and anarchy of the twentieth century. A clear evidence of his states-

---

[1] Envoys to Naples, Turin, and Spain respectively. —Ed.

manship was his effort to meet this danger by attempting to preserve the unity of the great powers, by espousing a principle of intervention against revolution, and by promoting the beginnings of a confederation of Europe. Whatever the shortcomings of Metternich's outlook on domestic issues, in other words, his program was genuinely and constructively European.

Certainly there is something to this thesis. That is, Metternich was undoubtedly "European" in a sense that Palmerston or Clemenceau was not. He valued five-power unity and international accord and could never bring himself, as Canning did, to rejoice that the era of congresses was over and that the old politics of national ambition and balance of power were back in vogue. It is, I feel, important to keep in mind the fact that Metternich was an early-nineteenth-century aristocratic internationalist in outlook, not a twentieth-century democratic one. There were definite limitations to Metternich's Europeanism; self-interest and class interest played a definite role in shaping it. By "Europe" he generally meant only the five great powers and their machinery of state. The European society and civilization which he claimed to defend are hardly distinguishable from the narrow, highly aristocratic society within which he ruled and prospered. The dangers he foresaw were not those of totalitarian democracy and total war, but simply those of successful middle-class revolution, which represented for him the great abyss, beyond which all was dark and incalculable. The impending chaos, anarchy, and dissolution of society against which he so incessantly warned meant simply the overthrow of absolute monarchy and aristocratic rule in favor of constitutions, representative government, and middle-class predominance. Yet all the limitations in Metternich's interna-

tional outlook do not deny him the status of a genuine nineteenth-centrury European. No one could expect him, in his time, to be a Robert Schuman or a Paul-Henri Spaak. Certainly he saw clearly that the conservative ideals and social order he represented were European and international in character and scope, and had to be defended on an international basis. Too much importance has been attached, in my opinion, to Metternich's statement, "Europe has for a long time held for me the significance of a fatherland," but it does contain a kernel of truth.

It is one thing to recognize that Metternich's outlook was European. It is quite another, however, to argue that his *policy* in this period was also European, i.e., that his chief aims were the maintenance of five-power unity and the promotion of European principles and institutions in the direction of a confederation of Europe. There is, in my opinion, no real evidence to sustain this latter contention, and a good deal of evidence pointing in the opposite direction. One can demonstrate quite clearly that Metternich consistently followed a policy of defending and advancing his country's interests (as, of course, any statesman must). That he was willing at any time to sacrifice, subordinate, or even de-emphasize Austrian interests to maintain European unity or advance European goals appears doubtful.

He was not, for instance, ready to make sacrifices to maintain the unity of the Concert of Powers. To picture Metternich as struggling in vain to hold the alliance together against the separatist tendencies of England and France is, in my view, a serious misconception. However much Metternich talked about allied harmony and exhorted England and France to adhere to the common cause, the fact is that he deliberately chose a policy which he knew would drive at least one of them, and possibly both, out of the alliance, because this policy would enable him to form a separate, intimate coalition with Russia and Prussia more suitable for Austrian interests.

This is the precise significance of Metternich's adoption of the Russian intervention principle at Troppau. Metternich knew that England could tolerate neither a change in the purpose of the existing alliance nor an extension of the commitments of existing treaties. Both Metternich and Gentz agreed in principle with Castlereagh's interpretation of the alliance, and used much the same arguments as he in criticizing Capodistrias' memoir of November 2 at the Congress. Yet once Matternich had succeeded in making Russian policy thoroughly conservative instead of mildly liberal, he not only was willing to accept the intervention principle he had formerly repudiated, but even to propose a new general treaty which would place all European governments under great-power supervision, guaranteeing them, through the great-power right of intervention, against any illegal change. This proposal of Metternich's represented so drastic a change in the purpose of the alliance and so sweeping an extension of alliance commitments that even the Russians were here unwilling to follow him.

Such a policy meant, of course, breaking all ties with England. It must be emphasized that this was a deliberate, conscious choice on Metternich's part. He knew that he was separating Austria from England and France and creating a separate coalition with aims different from those of the general alliance, because a close union with Russia and Prussia was worth far more to Austria than the general alliance, with its mere outward show of

great-power unity, could possibly be. He therefore counted the achievement of this union, despite its bad results for the alliance, as one of his greatest achievements. He wrote to Bubna at the Congress of Laibach:

As long as we could not strike in the first four weeks [after the outbreak of the Neapolitan revolution] we had to seek strong moral supports for ourselves. These we have found. The close union with Russia—and in this matter it is both intimate and impossible to doubt—is a blessing which cannot be sufficiently valued. England is dead so far as the Continent is concerned; France, more than uncertain. If I have accomplished anything, it is this: to have united [*verbruedert*] *all our neighbors* with us. Once [they are] bound and *compromised* on a matter of this sort, their retreat is no longer possible. Who would have believed that Austria could march in a moral union with Russia and Prussia, with Germany and all the Italian princes? Did not all the calculations of the liberals go against this?

The breach with England which Metternich here accepted as a small price to pay for Russian support was, to be sure, partly healed when their common interests in the Russo-Turk crisis served to bring Austria and England together. A second rift split them again at Verona, however, this time for good, and for the same reason that had arisen at Troppau. Forced to choose between a close union with Russia on the basis of a general intervention principle and cooperation with England on the basis of the letter and intent of the original alliance, Metternich chose Russia.

As for France, in 1820–1821 she also repudiated the Austro-Russian intervention principle, though less vigorously than England. In 1822–1823, however, France discovered that she could adapt the intervention policy and the Austrian example in Italy to her own ends in Spain. Thus the effect of Metternich's policy was also to help launch France on a course independent of the alliance in foreign affairs.

Unquestionably, alliance unity would have broken down sooner or later anyway. The whole trend of the times was against it; Canning and Villèle[2] would eventually have followed independent policies regardless of what Metternich said or did. Yet this does not alter the fact that, far from struggling to maintain the unity of the alliance at all costs, Metternich was the first to break away from it and to form a separate bloc of states to advance Austrian interests. The independent policies pursued by the western powers were in part reactions to the separatist policy already begun by Austria.

Nor can Metternich's espousal of the intervention principle be regarded as evidence of a policy of European social conservatism, as has sometimes been argued. Quite apart from the fact that the principle served to divide Europe into two opposed camps, it is plain that Metternich's attitude toward intervention, both in theory and application, was strictly opportunistic. He opposed the doctrine of intervention, both on theoretical and practical grounds, up to November 7, 1820; thereafter he defended it with arguments that were often directly contrary to those he had used before. As for the actual application of the principle, Metternich opposed intervention to suppress four of the six European revolutions which broke out in this period. Only in regard to Naples and Piedmont did he invoke the intervention principle to justify an Austrian intervention designed to protect strictly Austrian interests. The conclusion is unmistakable: Metternich tailored his principles on intervention to suit the political exigencies of the moment. As the

friend of England, he opposed a principle of intervention; as the friend of Russia, he adopted it. Where Austrian interests were at stake, he used it; outside the sphere of Austrian hegemony, he tried to prevent its use.

It is equally difficult to see European principles or federative polity in the institutions which Metternich attempted to establish. Whatever the German Confederation and the abortive Italian League might conceivably have led to in the way of European confederation, they were assuredly not intended by Metternich as means to this end. Indeed, their purpose was just the opposite—to reinforce an exclusively Austrian hegemony in Central Europe, and to prevent German or Italian unification or federation. Two other Metternichean ideas which might be construed as leading toward European confederation—his various proposals for great-power supervision of smaller states and his repeated attempts to establish a joint information center at Vienna—are equally devoid of real European sentiment. Whether the enlarging of the sovereignty of three autocratic states at the expense of numerous small ones or the erection of an international antirevolutionary secret-police and spy system represent steps toward European confederation, others may decide; certainly Metternich valued these devices solely as weapons against revolution and political change. It is, moreover, important to realize that Metternich proposed these ideas knowing that they would not unite Europe but would split it even further into two contending camps. Not only England and France, but also other constitutional states—Sweden, the Netherlands, Switzerland, and possibly the South German states—would certainly have opposed an international antirevolutionary information center. As for Metternich's principle

---

[2] Count Joseph de Villèle, French premier.—Ed.

of intervention, no small state, constitutional or absolutist, could have been fully confortable with it. Had either of these ideas ever really been effected, the result would have been a sharpening of the division of Europe into two spheres—the autocracies of the East and their satellites versus the constitutional West.

Nor do some of Metternich's diplomatic practices conform to the picture of the European statesman concerned to promote harmony among the powers. However much he proclaimed to France that Austria had no intention of trying, in the old discredited manner, to create a sphere of influence in Italy, his persistent efforts to reinforce and extend Austrian hegemony in Italy were bound to produce the conviction in France that this was exactly what Austria was doing. Metternich's practice of sowing suspicion and distrust between different powers in the Concert in order to align one or the other power more closely with Austria was likewise hardly conducive to Allied unity. In 1819–1820 Metternich exerted himself to make the English government suspicious of Russia, supplying Castlereagh with copious information on alleged Russian intrigues in Europe, Persia, India, and the Ionian Isles, then under British rule. In 1821–1823, however, he was equally zealous about informing Alexander of the revolutionary tendencies of British policy all over the world. At the Congress of Verona, finally, he carried off the virtuosic feat of arousing and maintaining Russian suspicion of France, French suspicion of Russia, and English suspicion of both France and Russia, all at the same time. In the same style, and of the same doubtful value to European solidarity, was Metternich's policy of attempting to unseat people he disliked from their posts within other governments. Some of the targets of his intrigues were, in England, Charles

Stuart, Lord Burghersh, and Canning; in France, the Duke of Dalberg, La Tour du Pin, and Pasquier; in Prussia, Humboldt and Hardenberg; and in Russia, Tatistchev, Stroganov, Pozzo di Borgo, and Capodistrias.

One need not moralize about these practices. Only when Metternich is presented as the European statesman *par excellence* and the assertion is made and repeated that Europe and the unity of the alliance were uppermost in his thought and action do these aspects of his diplomacy become hard to understand. For they are precisely the sort of practices which Castlereagh, for one, sought to avoid because he believed they were detrimental to Allied unity. When, however, Metternich is seen primarily as an Austrian diplomat with Austrian interests to defend, these practices become wholly understandable, if not admirable, tools of his trade. Indeed, there is not a single major aspect of his policy in this period which is not best and most simply understood as an effort to secure power, peace, and internal security for the fragile Austrian monarchy. In his correspondence with Stadion and others Metternich sometimes says as much. His remarkable success in achieving his goals under the guise of European principles, and not the validity or the sincerity of the principles themselves, constitutes his own particular brand of greatness.

The third basic question, "Was Metternich a conservative?" is probably the most difficult to answer, precisely because of the wealth of definitions and connotations which the word "conservative" bears. If one defines as conservative any philosophy or policy which identifies itself with the existing order and seeks to maintain it, then Metternich was certainly a conservative, and indeed the outstanding representative of conservatism in his time. If, however, one tries to distinguish between policies of conservatism, standstillism, and reaction, the question becomes much more complicated. For according to the commonplace definitions of a liberal as one who welcomes change in society and tries to promote it, a conservative as one who accepts change and tries to restrain and guide it, a "stand-patter" as one who resists change and tries to retain what exists unchanged, and a reactionary as one who rejects change and tries to re-store an order already past, Metternich's policy appears in this period to be occa-sionally one of reaction,[3] usually one of standstillism, and seldom if ever one of conservatism. To use the German terms for which there seem to be no precise En-glish equivalents, his was a policy of *Be-harren*, not *Erhaltung*.

That Metternich's policy during this era was essentially a negative, repressive one of resistance to change has already been argued at some length. The only point which might be added to that thesis here is that this policy does not seem to have been only a temporary expedient forced upon Metternich by the revolu-tionary events of the time, but rather to have been coherent with his general out-look. It is impossible to avoid the im-pression that Metternich equated change and reform with subversion and revolu-tion. He viewed the world in Zoroastrian terms as an arena of perpetual struggle between two world-governing principles, that of order and good versus that of evil and anarchy. Every existing right was not merely legitimate but holy (a favorite Metternichean phrase is "the sanctity of all existing rights"); every call for change or attempt at change made by anyone

except a legitimate sovereign was not merely illegitimate but wickedly pre-sumptuous. All the good men of right principles, sound reasoning, loyalty, and courage were on Metternich's side; only knaves, malcontents, and fools were on the other. All liberals, however moderate, were really revolutionaries; all demands for a constitution or for reforms, however limited, were really steps toward anarchy and revolution; all attacks upon the exist-ing order, whatever their nature, were plots fomented by the Central Revolu-tionary Committee in Paris. Now one may make many allowances in appraising statements like this, encountered so fre-quently in Metternich's writings. One may attribute the moral fervor and the evangelistic ardor of his denunciations to the purposes of rhetoric and propaganda. One may account for the sweeping and dogmatic character of his assertions as the result of his tendency toward exaggera-tion, or of his propensity for clear-cut, rigid categories and classifications. Yet when every possible allowance has been made, it is only fair to Metternich to rec-ognize that there is a substantial kernel of conviction beneath the husk of extrav-agant language. He was neither wholly cynical nor wholly self-deceived. Ulti-mately, he really believed that it was by preventing change and by preserving the *status quo* that he could do the most good in saving society.

Once again, one may readily grant that Metternich was not alone in this philos-ophy of state. He was doubtless the most distinguished of a whole host of sover-eigns, ministers, and theorists who be-lieved and argued as he did. His kind of thinking has persisted through revolu-tions and wars down to the present day. The only claim I am unwilling to grant is that Metternich's views represent any genuine conservative philosophy worthy

---

[3] While I believe Metternich's policy may on occa-sion be legitimately termed "reactionary," the word bears such an ineradicable bad moral connotation that I intend to avoid its use where possible.

of being compared with that of Edmund Burke, for example. His "system" was something else again—a wholehearted adherence to the *status quo* in principle, and a supple, stubborn, but ultimately hopeless defense of it in practice.

There are, to be sure, several considerations which appear to give the lie to this theory and to demonstrate in Metternich a greater flexibility in outlook than I have conceded. It might be argued that Metternich insisted he opposed not change *per se,* but only uncontrolled—hence revolutionary—change. He was no rigid absolutist, for he praised the British constitution and could at least tolerate constitutions in France and South Germany. Neither was he an inflexible legitimist, for he sometimes ignored or tampered with the principle of legitimacy, and nursed a secret admiration for the great usurper, Napoleon.

All these statements are true enough, and demonstrate that Metternich was not, in Grillparzer's[4] phrase, "the Don Quixote of legitimacy," who spent his life fighting phantoms and tilting at windmills. There is certainly a great gulf fixed between Metternich and the monarchs with whom and with whose cause he was identified. But the difference between himself and a Ferdinand I, a Charles X, a Charles Felix, or a Francis I lay in Metternich's greater intelligence, suppleness, and common sense, not in any fundamental difference in outlook. Closely examined, the evidences for his flexibility prove only that he knew when and how to yield to the power of circumstances—and he could never have been the great diplomat that he was without a mastery of this art. Beyond this, these evidences prove nothing.

---

[4] Franz Grillparzer, Austrian dramatist and critic. —Ed.

The fact that Metternich sometimes conceded in principle the admissibility of political change (as in the proposed Act of Guarantee at Troppau) does not bear great weight, first of all because, as has already been argued, the whole role of principles in his policy is a dubious one. He rode roughshod over several of what he claimed were his most sacred principles in his dealings with Ferdinand I and Naples, while displaying on other occasions an ingenious but logically questionable facility for drawing two exactly opposite conclusions from one and the same principle to suit different needs. Not rancor or prejudice, then, but a prudent skepticism warns one against leaning heavily on a Metternichean statement of principle unless it has been translated into practice.

And precisely this did not happen. Theoretically, Metternich conceded the admissibility of change, provided that it was initiated from above by the legitimate sovereign (a right, incidentally, which a legitimist could hardly deny to a monarch). In practice, however, this theoretical admission played no role at all in Metternich's policy. His private counsel to every sovereign was to make no changes at all in fundamental institutions, and all other changes only in the interest of repressing agitation and revolution. He counted it a positive virtue of the Italian sovereigns, even before the 1820 revolutions, that they made no innovations at all, and he did his utmost at Laibach and Verona to take away their right to make innovations in the future. At best, Metternich's principle would have reserved the right to initiate changes solely to those least interested in making them; in actual practice he sought to reduce even these minimal chances of change to something approaching zero.

Metternich's theoretical admission of

legitimate, peaceful change, therefore does not really disprove the claim that his policy was one of standstillism; nor do his apparent concessions to constitutionalism make him less an absolutist. Certainly he accepted the British constitution so long as Great Britain and Austria were close partners—it would have been very foolish of him to attack it. The British constitution, he reasoned, was ancient and therefore real; all others were modern and hence artificial. Once the split betweeng England and Austria emerged at Laibach, however, a totally different appraisal of the British system appears in Metternich's dispatches, one consistent with the whole tenor of his other views and principles. Now he contended that England, because of her representative system and civil liberties, was on the road to becoming "the most dangerous enemy of repose and order which Europe will ever have faced." An important evil which Austria had to fight against, he maintained, "is the essentially false position in which the English monarchy finds itself since the revolution of 1688." The strain in Anglo-Austrian relations was simply the concomitant of a fundamental difference in system between a monarchy *de jure,* resting squarely on the right of prescription and legitimacy, and a monarchy which existed solely *de facto,* because it attempted to reconcile monarchical right with popular sovereignty. The most signal proof of the degeneration of English statesmanship was that even Castlereagh and Liverpool repudiated the ideas of divine right and passive obedience and argued for the existence of that chimerical monster, a justified revolution. According to Metternich, the Revolution in 1688 was, in reality, no revolution at all, but solely a legal development of the existing system, and "the mere idea of a revolution founded upon any right whatsoever has

never entered the head of any competent interpreter of the spirit and history of that [British] constitution."

Much more could be said about these and other similarly startling assertions, as well as the Cassandralike prophecies of England's impending doom which Metternich up to the time of his death never tired of proclaiming. But enough has been said to indicate that, whatever ideological kinship there may have existed between Metternich and a Lord Eldon or George IV, he was certainly at heart far from being a true disciple of Edmund Burke.

As for the French *Charte,* during this period at least Metternich never approved of it in principle, but was reconciled to it only because any alternative to it (a Royalist *coup d'etat,* for example) was more dangerous than the *Charte* itself. He regarded the French as innately unfit for constitutional rule, requiring despotic rule like that of Napoleon. Far from breaking with the doctrine of legitimacy in regard to France, he argued that had the Allies not restored the Bourbon dynasty in France, all their glorious efforts would have been in vain, "for the first of all principles, . . . the foremost of all of society's interests [legitimacy], would not have been satisfied."

Nor does Metternich's admiration for Napoleon (a highly equivocal admiration, incidentally) change the general picture of his outlook. For the Napoleon whom Metternich admired was a divine-right legitimist at heart, who regretted "not being able to invoke the principle of legitimacy as the basis of his power," and who hoped some day himself to assume the title of "Holy" which the Austrian Emperor had officially laid down. What made Napoleon great in Metternich's eyes was his conquest of the revolution, his subjection of the masses, and his ability, while being himself indifferent to religious practices, to use and appreciate religion, particularly Catholicism, as the basis for government and the source of order. In short, Metternich showed a leaning for neither the reformer nor the conqueror in Napoleon, but for the cynical and successful despot with a strong penchant for legitimacy and order— someone, that is, not far removed from Metternich himself.

No evidence, therefore, tells seriously against the view that Metternich's political theory in this period was that of absolutism, complete with divine right and passive obedience. However much he spoke of "tempered monarchy" and ancient forms, it altered in no way his insistence that all power in the state belonged indivisibly and inalienably to the king, the sole divinely-ordained source of all authority, against whose will there could be no possible justified resistance or revolt. No advisory bodies could exist, no ministers function in the state other than at the royal pleasure. Liberty meant simply the freedom of the king's will; autocratic governments were therefore free governments and constitutional regimes were *ipso facto* unfree. The national will was the will of the sovereign. Kings were made to govern, and people to be governed. Two things, to be ruled firmly and to enjoy material prosperity, represented the sum total of popular capabilities, needs, and aspirations. "The mass of the people," remarked Metternich, citing Napoleon as his authority, "is always inert; they suffer their burdens in silence; and material benefits are regarded and enjoyed by them as well-being."

It bears repeating that no one need become exercised over this rather cynical but commonly-held doctrine of the early nineteenth century. It is so little surprising that Metternich shared it that the point would scarcely be worth making had not the rehabilitation of Metternich proceeded to the point where some would make of him a political philosopher with conservative principles of timeless validity. Against this tendency, it may be useful to point out once more that Metternich was basically a rigid absolutist whose political outlook was tied to a system of government and society which may once have had its grandeur and fitness, but which even by Metternich's time was becoming outworn, and by our own is completely anachronistic. It does Metternich no good service to take very seriously his boastful claims to modernity. His famous lament that he was born in the wrong century and would have been better off seeing the light of day either a century earlier or later is only partly justified. In the seventeenth or eighteenth century, he would certainly have been at home. In his own age, he achieved undeniable stature, perhaps even greatness, as the outstanding representative and defender of a dying order. But in the twentieth century, he could only have been a Von Papen.

To say all this is certainly not to return to Metternich as the blind monster sometimes portrayed in nineteenth-century historiography, or even Viktor Bibl's[5] more recent "demon of Austria," a Metternich without a single redeeming quality, responsible for everything that has gone wrong with Austria since 1809. No one can deny to Metternich the virtues of moderation, caution, and love of peace, nor the qualities of courage (in his own way) and outstanding diplomatic skill. Often his diplomacy was very successful; sometimes his influence and policy worked for good, though on the whole their results for Austria and Europe were hardly good in the long run. Metternich

---

[5] Austrian historian. See below, p. 116.—Ed.

also must bear only part of the responsibility for the standstill policy followed by Austria. Certainly the character of Francis I, the peculiar makeup of the Habsburg Empire, and possibly even the folk characteristics of the Austrian people were factors of equal or greater importance. Finally, if it has any bearing, one may readily admit that the repressive policies of Metternich look very mild alongside the tyranny of a Hitler or Stalin. Tyranny, like most things, is much more highly developed and organized in the twentieth century—and Metternich was never a tyrant in the real sense of the word.

The only view to which one must return if the interpretation set out here is correct is something like that of Charles Dupuis, who contended early in the twentieth century that Metternich led the Concert of Europe more as a good Austrian than as a good European, and that this was an important factor in the system's decline. My own interpretation involves simply seeing Metternich, for this period at least, as less statesman than diplomat; as less European than Austrian; as less a constructive conservative than a repressive "standpatter"; as less profound and earnest than clever but essentially cynical and superficial; and also, perhaps, as less the philosopher-king and forerunner of European unity than the *grand seigneur,* outstanding in certain abilities but typical of his class in his general outlook, and dedicating his efforts to preserving and enjoying the old regime.

Believing that the purpose of history is to inspire in the service of a cause, HEINRICH VON TREITSCHKE (1834–1896) wrote unabashedly from a bitterly anti-Austrian viewpoint in order to show the necessity of German unification under Prussia. Despite this bias, his brilliant literary style and depth of research have given him a high place among German historians. The excerpt chosen here is from his most famous work, originally published between 1879 and 1894. Typically, it denies to Metternich's program of repression any higher motive than Austrian power politics in Germany.*

Heinrich von Treitschke

Reactionary Exploiter of Germany

On July 22nd, Metternich reached Carlsbad, inspired by the proud conviction that "from this place either the salvation or the ultimate destruction of the social order will proceed." Emperor Francis had abandoned a proposed visit to his Lombardo-Venetian kingdom because the repression of the German revolution seemed a more urgent matter. The intimates with whom the Austrian statesman first conversed were, in addition to Gentz, his two friends of the Vienna congress, the Hanoverians, Counts Hardenberg and Münster. In any case, in all matters where no intervention of parliament was to be feared, Metternich could unconditionally rely upon the highly reactionary sentiments of the tory cabinet, and subsequently he wrote gratefully to the prince regent: "One is always certain to find your royal highness on the road of sound principles." But all other assistance was worthless in default of an unconditional understanding with the crown of Prussia. In order to bring this about, Metternich hastened to Teplitz, and there, on July 29th, had a private conversation with King Frederick William, which determined the course of German policy for years to come. The king showed himself to be extremely discomposed on account of the sinister demagogic plans which, as Wittgenstein[1] assured him, had

---

[1] Prince Wilhelm von Wittgenstein, Prussian minister of police and collaborator of Metternich.—Ed.

*Taken from Heinrich von Treitschke, *Treitschke's History of Germany in the Nineteenth Century,* translated by Eden and Cedar Paul (7 vols.; New York: McBride, Nast and Company, 1915-1917), vol. III, pp. 206–214, 226–229. Footnotes omitted. Used by permission of Crown Publishers, Inc.

been disclosed by the latest domiciliary searches; he was annoyed, and with good reason, on account of the chancellor's inefficiency and dilatoriness of his ministry, which had kept him waiting seven months for an answer to urgent enquiries. He complained, "My own people fail me," and he committed himself confidingly to the advice of this Austrian who in Aix-la-Chapelle had already given him such admirable counsel. Metternich understood how to strike the iron while it was hot. For Prussia, he declared, the day had now arrived for a choice between the principle of conservatism and political death; the great conspiracy had its origin and its seat in Prussia, and it penetrated even the ranks of the highest officials; still everything could yet be saved if the crown would make up its mind not to grant any popular representation in the modern democratic sense of the term, and would content itself with estates. At the same time he handed in a memorial in which he repeated the ideas voiced by him at Aix-la-Chapelle. The king's assent to these proposals was a matter of course, for even Hardenberg's constitutional plan had never aimed at more than a representation of the three estates, and had not dreamed of a representation of the people as a whole.

Upon the monarch's orders, Hardenberg, Bernstorff,[2] and Wittgenstein now held confidential conversations with the Austrian. The chancellor laid his constitutional proposal before his Viennese friend, and secured the latter's complete approval. On August 1st, Hardenberg and Metternich signed a convention evidently drafted by Metternich, concerning the general principles of the federal policy of the two great powers. The convention was to be kept permanently secret owing to "the prejudices which inspire many of the German governments against a closer and most wholesome union between the two leading German courts." The parties to the convention went on to recall the constitutional aim of the Germanic Federation, as guaranteed by Europe; and then declared (article 2) that as European powers it was their duty to watch over the political existence of the Federation, while as German federal states it was their duty to care for the safety of the federal constitution. For this reason, within the interior of the Federation, no principles must be applied that were incompatible with its existence, and all decisions of the Bundestag[3] must be faithfully carried out as laws of the Federation. The article of the federal act which imposed upon the Federation the duty of caring for the internal safety of Germany, an article unquestionably intended solely to avert the danger of breaches of the public peace, thus received an entirely new and utterly arbitrary interpretation; it was to serve to subject to a uniform rule the internal affairs also of the federal states. Since the revolutionary party threatened the existence of all governments (thus proceeded the agreement) the present opportunity must be utilised in order to secure closer union among the German courts, and to establish at the Bundestag the rule of the majority. First of all, therefore, there must be an agreement about article 13 of the federal act—and here followed an astounding pledge which, as far as Metternich was concerned, constituted the kernel of the document. Article 7 ran as follows: "Prussia is resolved to apply this article in its literal sense to her own domains only after her

---

[2] Count Christian Bernstorff, Prussian foreign minister.—Ed.

[3] German name for federal diet, the assembly of the German Confederation.—Ed.

internal financial affairs shall have been fully regulated; that is to say, she is determined that for the representation of the nation she will not introduce any general system of popular representation incompatible with the geographical and internal configuration of her realm, but that she will give her provinces representative constitutions (*landständische verfassungen*), and will out of these construct a central committee of territorial representatives."

Naturally this clause involved a mutual pledge, for, beyond question, Emperor Francis was equally resolved not to introduce any general system of popular representation. Article 7 in essentials conveyed nothing new, for Hardenberg had long before resolved that the constitution should not be promulgated until after the completion of the new financial laws, which were now nearly ready; while the ordinance of May, 1815, expressly prescribed that territorial representation was to proceed from the provincial diets. All the more ignominious therefore was the form of the pledge. Like a repentant sinner, and without any formal counterpledge, the monarchy of Frederick the Great gave a foreign power a promise about the subsequent conduct of certain internal affairs whose control every self-respecting state should keep within its own hands; and Metternich reported with delight to his emperor that "Prussia has given an engagement not to concede any popular representation." This was the most shameful humiliation which Hardenberg had ever brought upon Prussia. The policy of peaceful dualism was now to be tested, and its outcome proved to be the subjection of Prussia to Austria's leadership. The chancellor signed the document because he saw no other way of retaining his king's shaken confidence; and because the promise, taken literally,

certainly contained nothing which ran counter to the hitherto accepted principles of Prussian policy. But both parties to the agreement cherished hidden designs. By the term "central committee," Hardenberg, as he was soon to show, understood a large national Landtag, whereas Metternich, now, as before in Aix-la-Chapelle, was thinking only of a small committee of about one-and-twenty members, and secretly hoped that even this shadow of a Prussian central administration (of which his emperor was extremely afraid) might yet be prevented from coming into existence. Thus Prussia had completely come over to the side of the new Viennese doctrine, in accordance with which article 13 promised representation of estates merely, and not popular representatives. Both the powers pledged themselves "to assist those states which (under the name of estates) have already introduced systems of popular representation, to return to methods better adapted to the Federation," and, with this end in view, to await first of all the proposals of the governments concerned.

The press was the second object of the Carlsbad deliberations. The two great powers were agreed regarding the principles of a memorial by Gentz, which described in the most emphatic language how, in view of the equality in civilisation in the different states, and the complex circumstances of intercourse among the Germans, no individual state could preserve itself from infection, and how, therefore, every prince who tolerated press licence within his own land committed high treason against the Federation. For this reason a strict federal press law was essential, and, above all, "the German governments must mutually pledge themselves that none of the editors who have become notorious to-day are to be allowed to undertake the editorship of new papers, and, generally speaking, must pledge themselves to reduce as far as possible the number of newspapers."

The third topic for the conference was the universities and the schools. Metternich had a very low estimate of the political capacity of the professors, basing this judgment, characteristically enough, upon the opinion that no professor knew how to pay due regard to the value of property; but he considered the political activity of these unpractical people to be indirectly most dangerous, because they taught "the union of the Germans to constitute a single Germany," and because the rising generation was being brought up "to pursue this insane aim." It was for this reason that he laid so much stress upon the speedy dismissal of demagogic teachers, and Hardenberg was weak enough to throw overboard forthwith all the reasonable principles of that memorial by Eichhorn[4] which Count Bernstorff had only a few days before sent to the Bundestag. He agreed to the stipulation "that professors whose sentiments are notoriously bad, and who are involved in the intrigues of the disorderly students of to-day, shall immediately be deprived of their chairs, and that no one who is thus dismissed from any German university shall be reappointed to a university in any other German state." Finally, it was arranged that the same rules should be extended to the teachers in the schools.

Such were the contents of this unhappy convention. It seemed as if a sinister destiny presided over this unfortunate nation which was so laboriously striving to emerge from its state of disintegration, forbidding to it all possibility of self-understanding, forcibly imposing barriers in the way of any advance towards political power. Many of the disastrous

aberrations of the German patriots in later years are explicable solely out of the absolute confusion of all political ideas which was the necessary outcome of the unnatural alliance of the two great powers. It was the aim of the two powers to provide for the authority of the Germanic Federation a reinforcement which was beyond question urgently needed: but they enlarged the competence of the Federation far beyond the prescriptions of the federal act; they allowed it a right of intervention into the internal affairs of the individual states, a right of intervention incompatible with the nature of a federation of states; they even spoke of felony on the part of German princes against the Federation, as if sovereignty by Napoleon's grace had already been annihilated, and as if the majesty of the old empire had been re-established. This "unitarian" policy, however, did not originate out of nationalist sentiment, but out of Austrian particularism. The Germanic Federation was to receive the authoritative powers of a sovereign state in order to annul for all time the desire of the Germans "to unite themselves to form a single Germany"; in order that the spiritual slumber of the peoples of Austria might continue undisturbed by the higher civilisation and the more lively spiritual energies of their German neighbours. In the most definite terms possible, acting upon repeated commands from his monarch, Metternich declared that he desired to save the Germanic Federation by Austrian co-operation, or, failing this, to separate the Austrian states from Germany, in order to save Austria by herself—and there was not yet to be found in the German nation a single mind to realise the unspeakable good fortune such a separation would be, or to voice the liberating cry, "Let us separate from Austria!"

---

[4] Johann Albrecht Eichhorn, Prussian minister and member of the state council.—Ed.

The means employed to further this policy were as corrupting and as un-German as were the aims of those who initiated it. The Germanic Federation did not as yet possess either a federal army or a federal supreme court, or indeed any kind of universally national institution except the Bundestag; and such a Federation, which could not even protect the Germans against the foreign world, was now (according to the wording of the Teplitz convention), "in the purest spirit of the Federation," to be empowered to disturb by prohibitions and prosecutions the holy of holies of the nation of Martin Luther, the free movement of ideas. Thus German policy sank, as it was aptly phrased, to the level of a German police system; for decades the entire life of the Bundestag was devoted to urgency police measures. The natural opposition between the absolutist centralised authority and the constitutional member-states became accentuated to the degree of irreconcilable enmity; anyone who would not abandon belief in political freedom was henceforward compelled to fight the German Bundestag, and thus the liberal party, although this party almost alone had grasped the idea of national unity with enthusiasm, was forced unwittingly and unwillingly into the arms of particularism. At the congress of Vienna all parties had felt that there must be conceded to the nation some of the "rights of Germanism," that from the side of the Federation a certain moderate degree of political liberty must be guaranteed, and it was only because the arrogance of Rhenish Confederate sovereignty made it impossible to secure an agreement about this minimum that the federal act had gone no further than to make promises expressed in very general terms. Now, all at once, everything was turned topsy-turvy. It was held that upon the Federa-tion devolved, not the smallest possible, but the greatest possible measure of political rights. No longer was the Federation to be the citadel of the nation's freedom, but it was to prescribe limits which the Landtags,[5] the press, and the universities were never to exceed. With what unprecedented frivolity, too, was it proposed to rob of their legal rights "the editors who are to-day in ill-repute, the notoriously disaffected teachers"—as if the arbitrary powers of the Committee of Public Safety to deal with suspects were to be renewed upon the peaceful soil of Germany!

What was the cause of this sinister mistrust felt for a loyal and law-abiding people? The Landtags of Bavaria and Baden, in the zeal of youthful inexperience, had brought forward a few foolish proposals; and yet at this very time the docile conduct of the Würtemberg estates showed that it was merely necessary for the governments to draw the reins a little tighter in order to control the presumption of their harmless popular representatives. The press, again, had sinned gravely by its aimless blustering and scolding, nor was Gentz entirely wrong in what he said in his memorial concerning the misbehaviour of the journals. "Today," he wrote, "there is not in Germany a single newspaper published as the outcome of private enterprise which those of the right way of thinking can regard as their organ, and this is a state of affairs which was unprecedented during the time of bloodiest anarchy in France." But beyond question, in Germany the press did not represent public opinion; the mass of the nation by no means shared the indignation expressed by the journalists; and anyone familiar with the German

---

[5] German name for state diets or sometimes, as in Austria, for provincial diets. How to define the term was part of the controversy of that time.—Ed.

fondness for fault-finding could unhesi-tatingly venture to prophesy that the great majority of German newspapers would always be on the side of the opposi-tion. It is true that the inadequate manner in which so many cultured men expressed their condemnation of Kotzebue's assas-sination showed that a portion of the higher classes had begun to despair of the existing order; but unquestionably a policy of blind and rough persecution was the best means to increase this despair. Finally, the revolutionary follies of the students certainly needed the strong hand; but they were restricted to three or four universities, and, even in these, in-volved no more than small circles; while if the universities were to be officially stigmatised as the nurseries of treason, the only result would be to drive the patriotic spirit of the young men into devious courses.

The worst feature of all was that the state which had restored freedom to Ger-many, the one which had everything to hope from national unity and nothing to dread, now voluntarily put its neck under the yoke of the Austrian dominion, and therefore, to that portion of the na-tion which could not see beyond the next day, assumed the semblance of a sworn enemy. The star of the Frederician state had become obscured by clouds of suspi-cion. By the anxious mood of a noble monarch misled by blind counsellors, and through the perplexities of the aging Hardenberg, this state had been diverted from the paths in which it had risen to greatness, and when Austria had gathered in the Teplitz harvest Metternich de-clared with satisfaction to the Russian envoy, "Prussia has ceded us a place which many Germans had designed for Prussia herself!"

As soon as the two great powers had come to an unreserved agreement, the victory of Austrian policy was decided. No one in the Carlsbad assembly was pre-pared to oppose them on principle. Count Schulenberg, the Saxon, now made com-mon cause with the two Hanoverians, for he, like them, was a strict advocate of the feudal state-system. Baron von Plessen, of Mecklenburg, a man of far more liberal and mobile intelligence, was by the traditions of his homeland forced into more or less the same position. Even the representatives of the so-called consti-tutional states manifested uncritical docility. Count Rechberg, the true orig-inator of the Bavarian plan for a *coup d'état,* did, indeed, in accordance with the custom of Munich, cherish some mis-trust for Austria; but he was far more afraid of the revolution, and this latter fear decided his conduct, although he had been expressly instructed not to ap-prove anything which infringed Bavarian sovereignty or the Bavarian constitution. Baron von Berstett gave such terrible accounts of the disorders of the Carls-ruhe representative assembly that in Gentz's opinion to listen to him was at once a horror and a delight. Marschall of Nassau outbid even the reactionary fanaticism of the Badenese statesman; nor did Count Wintzingerode leave any-thing to be desired in respect of hostility towards the demagogues, although to him was allotted the thorny task of avoiding anything that might completely under-mine the reputation of the most ex-emplary of constitutional kings.

The members of the Carlsbad assembly fortified one another in their fears of the great conspiracy, and Metternich was able to handle them so adroitly that Bern-storff wrote to the chancellor, "We can settle everything here, but later it will be impossible!" So completely did they adopt the Austrian view of German affairs that at length they all came to believe that they were doing a great and good work, and honestly rejoiced in the fine patriotic unity of the German crowns. "The issue lies in God's hand," wrote Bernstorff when their work had been completed; "but at any rate a great thing has already been achieved in that amid the storms of the time the German princes have been able to express their principles and intentions openly, definitely, and unanimously." The sense of satisfaction was all the stronger because the German statesmen were working entirely among themselves, and no foreign power even attempted to exercise any influence over the Carlsbad negotiations. As yet no one dreamed that this fine spectacle of national independence and harmony was nothing else than the subjection of the German nation to the foreign dominion of Austria. . . .

The four laws were all approved, and whatever was still lacking in respect of the interpretation of article 13 could easily be postponed until the Vienna conferences, which were to be held in November, for all parties were agreed upon "the maintenance of the monarchical principle." Even an enlargement of the rights of the majority at the Bundestag, such as had been planned by the two great powers in Teplitz, could perhaps also be secured in Vienna. The results exceeded all Metternich's expectations. "Never," he declared, "have more exemplary harmony and urbanity prevailed than at our conferences." When all met once more, on September 1st, to take leave of one another, everyone was in a good humour, and one of the ministers was so extremely enthusiastic that he proposed to his colleagues that they should sing the Ambrosian hymn of praise. Naturally, at the close of "this ever memorable meeting," the master of statecraft who had conducted affairs so admirably was hailed with the united expression of unbounded respect and gratitude, and due praise

was also given to the great talents of Councillor Gentz. A wonderful amount had, in fact, been accomplished in a few days. This cumbrous federation, which seemed inapt for any development, suddenly, and with revolutionary impetuosity, grasped political rights which had never been allotted to the ancient empire; it arrogated to itself dominion even over branches of internal political life which the powerful centralised authority of the modern German Empire leaves to the territories without restriction; so recklessly did it transgress the limits of its fundamental law that clear-sighted professors of constitutional law like Albrecht were able to maintain that after the Carlsbad decrees the Germanic Federation had abandoned the character of a federation of states, and had become transformed into a federal state—a view shared by many of Metternich's sympathisers, and especially by Ancillon. Without opposition, Germany's princes allowed all these limitations of their sovereignty to be imposed upon them by Austria. Metternich wrote in triumph: "If the emperor doubts being emperor of Germany he greatly deceives himself."

Never since Prussia had existed as a great power, never since the days of Charles V and Wallenstein, had the house of Austria been able to set foot so heavily upon the neck of the German nation. Just as masterfully as in former days Emperor Charles had imposed the Interim of Augsburg upon the contentious Reichstag of the conquered Schmalkaldians, so now did Metternich call a halt to a new national movement of the Germans; just as contemptuously as Granvelle had at that time laughed at the *peccata Germaniae*, so did Gentz now mock at the tribulations of the Old Bursch of Weimar and his liberal train; and just as submissively as in those days the weakly Joachim II, so now did a Hohenzollern stand before the Austrian ruler. But Austria had soon to learn that the crown which Emperor Francis had once torn from his own head was not to be regained by the trickeries of a false diplomacy. In earlier days Austria's dominion had always been a misfortune to the Germans; the more brightly the star of the Hapsburgs shone, the more prostrate was the condition of the German nation. That great emperor who, in Augsburg, had once desired to control Protestantism, had at any rate offered the Germans something to replace their lost freedom, a mighty thought, one capable of filling even a Julius Pflugk with enthusiasm, the great conception of the Catholic world-empire. But what could they offer to the nation, these petty spirits who now endeavoured to tread in the footsteps of Emperor Charles? Nothing but oppression and coercion, nothing but an unscrupulous distortion of the federal law, which must inevitably make their solitary national institution loathsome to the Germans, throwing as makeweight into the scale the lie that Germany was to be rescued from an imaginary danger.

For the real interests of the nation Metternich had nothing but a mocking smile. An exhortation from the minor courts regarding the unfulfilled pledge for the facilitation of commercial intercourse throughout Germany was met by the Austrian statesmen with empty phrases. He had had to promise the Prussian minister that the odious dispute regarding the federal fortresses should at length be brought to a close. Upon Prussia's demand, too, Langenau and Wolzogen[6] had already appeared in Carlsbad, the latter to the alarm of the strict Austrian party, who regarded him with suspicion as an emissary

[6] Baron Friedrich Karl von Langenau and Baron Ludwig von Wolzogen represented Austria and Prussia respectively on the Military Commission of the German Federation.—Ed.

of the German revolutionaries. But amid so many more important matters, Metternich found no time for the promised discussion with the two generals. Moreover, in relation to his policy, what mattered the safeguarding of the German frontiers when compared with the great civilising tasks of the censorship and the prosecution of the students? And since the new rulers of Germany were incomparably smaller and of less account than had been the Hapsburg heroes of the days of Schmalkald and of the Thirty Years' War, since these new rulers owed their successes, not to the might of victorious arms, but solely to the foolish terrors of the German courts, the inevitable reaction set in, not, as in the days of Maurice and Gustavus Adolphus, firmly and forcibly, but slowly, unnoticed—and yet all the more certainly. Austria had offered the Germans a stone in place of bread. As soon as Prussia determined to deal honourably with the needs of this nation, and to provide that economic unity which Prussia alone could give, from that moment the spectre of German dualism, whose hideous features had once again been displayed, began gradually to fade, and the thinking part of the nation came gradually to realise that the withdrawal of Austria from the Germanic Federation, so arrogantly threatened in Carlsbad, offered the only possible means of rescuing the fatherland.

But this prospect was still remote. At the moment, the Hofburg was jubilant with victory. In an affectionate autograph note, Emperor Francis thanked the king of Prussia for his vigorous common action "against the disturbers of that established order upon which the existence of the thrones depends." Gentz sang the glories of "the greatest step backwards which has been made in Europe for thirty years," and to the Austrian envoy in London Metternich expressed the hope that this deed of salvation would find an echo throughout Europe. In actual fact, in Spain alone had the ideas of pure reaction hitherto secured so decisive a success. Among the great civilised nations it was Germany which first gave the example of a *coup d'état* from above, an example which eleven years later served as proto- type for the July ordinances in France. The policy of moderation which the Quadruple Alliance had observed down to the time of the congress of Aix-la-Chapelle, was now at an end; the power which had acquired the leading position in the European alliance openly mani- fested itself on the side of the principles of oppression.

In contrast to Treitschke, HEINRICH RITTER VON
SRBIK, in this second selection from his pen, presents
Metternich as a man sincerely worried about revolution
in Germany. Beyond that, however, even this champion
of Metternich finds it impossible to condone the
Carlsbad Decrees, concluding that they were, despite
lofty intentions, one of Metternich's most serious errors
of judgment. The excerpt is from the famous biography
previously mentioned.*

Heinrich Ritter von Srbik

Honest Leader Against Revolution

Today there is growing recognition that
the possibilities of a bourgeois political
revolution in Germany and, soon after,
even a social revolution, were by no
means negligible. Nevertheless, the dark-
est of shadows will ever and with justice
fall on the oft-described countermeasures
of these months: on the investigations of
the promoters of the Burschenschaft
movement, the persecution of professors
and students, the campaign in Prussia
against academic freedom, and Jahn's
gymnastic movement. Prussia's decision-
makers were again fully prepared psychologically to carry out Metternich's battle
plan against Jacobinism: Humboldt, only
recently appointed to the ministry, pow-
erless against Wittgenstein, Bernstorff,
Kamptz,[1] and Ancillon, and in barely
concealed opposition to Hardenberg;
the state chancellor, weak and himself
apprehensive about the revolution, as-
siduously defending his plan for a constitution and clinging to his office; the king,
filled with fear of the "great conspiracy."
Metternich the savior, once again the only
one who knew what he wanted, was received with open arms. In part following
the plan of Gentz and Adam Müller, he
persuaded the court in Berlin to by-
pass the slow-moving and indecisive
federal diet, which he had originally put

[1] Karl Christoph von Kamptz, reactionary writer
and Prussian official.—Ed.

*From Heinrich Ritter von Srbik, *Metternich, der Staatsmann und der Mensch* (3 vols.; Munich: Verlag
F. Bruckmann KG, 1925–1954), vol. 1 pp. 589–596, omitting the original footnotes. Translated by Keith Mostofi and Enno E. Kraehe.

into the foreground, and to reach agreement with Austria first. The universities, the press, and the plans for an all-Prussian representation could now be struck with a single blow.

The events are well enough known: the first prosecution of demagogues in Prussia, which affected men like Arndt and the brothers Welker and the trusty Jahn; Metternich's conference with the Prussian king, at Teplitz, in which he issued anew his warning against a "central representation"; and the Teplitz agreement in which Austria and Prussia doubtlessly violated the rights of their own creation, the German Confederation. Here they pledged themselves to a uniform course in the internal affairs of this confederation; to muzzling of the press by preventive censorship; to disciplining of the universities, which "are bringing up generations of revolutionaries," by means of investigating commissions and the dismissal of notoriously bad professors; and to the "correction of notions regarding Article 13 of the federal constitution," which had held out the prospect of introducing estate-type constitutions in all confederated states. And what a success for Metternich that he wrested from Hardenberg the promise that until the internal and financial conditions of the realm were definitively regulated, Prussia would not introduce an all-encompassing popular representation incompatible with its geographic and internal structure, but would grant its provinces only estate-type constitutions and on the basis of these form a central committee of territorial representatives! Thus did Metternich at Teplitz take advantage of the "weakness, in which everything in Prussia foundered, to obtain commitments." King Frederick William ordered that all the Prussian documents, even the most secret, be placed at the disposal of the Austrian minister; and Metternich, after reading the investigation files from Berlin, Karlsruhe, Darmstadt, and Nassau, was firmly convinced that a very extensive conspiracy was planning the overthrow of all German governments, the elimination of twenty-one German princes and the leading statesmen, and that most of the higher state officials in Prussia and several leaders of the estates in various German states were involved in the conspiracy, which had its centers in the universities, especially Jena, Heidelberg, Giessen, and Freiburg. The majority of German youth who had attended the universities since 1815 and all the gymnastic institutions of Jahn seemed to him to be carriers of the movement, with many professors standing behind them. In the officials who had been stationed in the Rhenish provinces of Prussia over the last few years, he saw for the most part "out and out men of the revolution," and the close ties between the German conspirators and the French radicals were proven to him beyond a doubt.

It has already been suggested that these assumptions, whose subjective substantiation cannot be doubted, were objectively by no means completely incorrect, however tarnished a source confidential reports may be. The "German Movement," which emanated from Jena and Giessen, fell more and more into a republican-revolutionary channel; ever greater was the number of those who worked toward a unified German republic. Karl Follen tried to instill republican ideas into the gymnastic institutions, whose creator, Jahn, was himself a constitutional monarchist even though he kindled the hatred of the student movement toward the "Kamptz and Schmalz boys." Adolf Ludwig Follen tried to make storm troops for the German revolution out of the gymnasts and to train farmers, townsmen, and above all young people for revolution. The "Blacks" were connected with the Hessian peasant unrest of the year 1819; there existed an alliance of German "demagogues" and French radicals; attempts to unite the liberals of different nations in common action were not lacking. The radical influences from the "German Societies" infiltrated the student body at Giessen; the subjective ethics of the philosopher Fries[2] had a radicalizing effect on the Giesseners, on the Follens, and on Sand. And in Jena the historian, Heinrich Luden, who both hated and admired Napoleon and was the bitter critic of the Rhenish Confederation, the first and second peace treaties of Paris, and the work of the Vienna congress, inflamed the students with his own burning ardor for Germany and freedom. For him, history and politics were indissolubly fused. The publisher of *Nemesis* taught that the national state was the best political form; he turned away from the humanitarian ideal of the French Revolution, to the stark idea of power politics and the egoism of the state; he came out for Prussian leadership toward Germanization and the new state; he preached the people's state instead of the coercive state; he lived and taught the philosophies of Rousseau and Herder, Fichte and Kant, and was at the same time a pioneer of German political realism in historiography and politics. He saw in the "constitutional or republican monarchy" absolutely the best form of state, and he stood, even if not unconditionally, on the ground of popular sovereignty, constitutionalism, and the freedom and equality of all citizens. The German Federal Act was a work of embarrassment and shame for this academic

teacher and publicist. In the Germany of the future there was to be no element of foreign nationality, and the great German powers were to be bound politically to and by the Confederation. Fulfillment of Article 13 of the Federal Act in the sense of representation on the model of the English constitution, the publication of parliamentary proceedings, freedom, the containment of Catholicism—all these demands were combined with the most determined rejection of the prevailing system. And finally, given the refusal of the authorities to act on the ideas of reform, Luden proclaimed the necessity and moral justification of the revolution to act on the idea.

Much of this may have been taken up and passed on by Luden's audience in a crude form. The participation of professors in the radicalization of student thought has been objectively established: fatherland and freedom, noblest of idealistic goals, were presented to the impressionable minds of the listeners, and many an overheated imagination dreamed and spoke of dagger and regicide and praised Sand's pious deed. But should one have generalized to such lengths as Metternich and his partisans did? From the diaries and activities of individuals one drew false conclusions about the majority, and Metternich went so far astray as to characterize men like Boyen as scoundrels, in the political sense, and to confuse their struggle toward the inner renewal of the nation, toward the unification and freedom of a monarchical Germany by lawful means, with the radicalism of immaturity. His concern about revolution was not the fear of a phantom, but it amounted to a loss of judgment and the wrong choice of means when he pressed for "the curbing of the press, the destruction of the Burschenschaften, the abolition of the constitutional system," these "beneficent

---

[2] Jakob Friedrich Fries, liberal philosopher at the University of Jena.—Ed.

measures for Germany." It was the duty of every orderly state to defend against the doubtlessly extensive concrete preparations for revolution, but the harsh persecution of the intellectual movement in its entirety was a fatal error.

The two German great powers vied with each other at the federal diet to act against the introduction of the representative systems, freedom of the press, and of other "Jacobin" institutions in the individual states and managed to have the diet refrain from taking the initiative in the execution of said Article 13 of the Federal Act. The emphasis was placed on "estate-type," not on "constitutions," and the article, whose phrasing was so vague, was so interpreted that in place of the modern right of petition only the old right of supplication and complaint was left standing, and in place of participation in legislation only the right of consultation and the formal approval of taxes remained. The supreme power in the state was to abide undivided with the monarch; the division of legislative power between prince and people in representative-constitutional states seemed to Metternich and his party to be incompatible with this principle. Even before the Carlsbad congress, Gentz had written the memorandum "On the Distinction between Estate-type and Representative Constitutions" as the basis for the most important point of Metternich's program, the abolition of representative constitutions. Constitutional and estate-type principles were placed in the sharpest opposition. The former were explained as the revolutionary offspring of the ideas of 1789, while popular representation, ministerial responsibility, publicizing of debates, and unlimited right of petition were represented as being incompatible with the first requisite of a monarchical form of government and as an expression of the

unhistorical and unnatural mania for leveling. Article 13 was interpreted in the sense of the old estate-type constitution, and popular sovereignty and separation of powers, in keeping with the prevailing view of the times, were equated with a representative constitution.

"With God's help I hope to defeat the German Revolution as I defeated the conqueror of the world"—thus had Metternich, full of haughty arrogance, written shortly before the Teplitz conference. The Carlsbad conferences, which extended for several weeks from August 1819 on, were to mark that victory. Even the shrewd recorder, Gentz, believed in fact that "the plans of the enemy were positively aimed at assassination and the total overthrow of society"; he saw "colossally increasing dangers"; and if Metternich, as "the soul of the whole, had rarely given greater proofs of energy, zeal, and skill," if he "works to the point of excess, works his brain shamefully, and speaks and writes so much that he must eventually fall into a certain confusion," as Gentz reports, then this at least speaks for Metternich's honest belief in the goodness of his cause, however much his letters at the same time show the presence of a satisfied vanity.

He was convinced that it was "a question of salvation or death for society"; he saw interconnected plots throughout Germany aimed at abolition of the monarchical form of state. He believed that the overthrow of all existing institutions was the goal of the gymnasts, the students, and the "notoriously wicked professors like Arndt, Jahn, Oken, and Schleiermacher," and was the purpose behind the manipulation of the masses by the "rabble of journalists" and by the clamor for fulfillment of Article 13. He imagined that the outbreak of revolution in the Darmstadt and Rhenish areas of Prussia was imminent, and likewise the proclamation of a Cis-Rhenish Republic with the aid of the "purely revolutionary Landwehr system[3] of Prussia," through which a goodly part of the populace had been armed. Loyal to his conviction that Austria, as the center of the Continent, could not tolerate a major revolution in Europe, he believed himself duty bound to set a barrier against the demagogic drive for limited, representative constitutions (which of course only lead to democracy) by interpreting Article 13 in the "strict sense" of estate-type constitutions. He was certain that the Grand Duke of Weimar was "implicated in the Sand affair"; he characterized Bavaria and Baden as states revolutionized by their constitutions, their popular deputies, and the publication of their debates; he viewed Württemberg as still involved in the struggle with the unavoidable consequences of "the purely demagogic principles of the pact between rulers and people"; and he thought that all three courts, being full of remorse about the disintegration of royal power, were already "in penitential garb seeking to find aid at the court which they daily insulted."

One is familiar with the press law of Carlsbad, which subjected all journals and books under twenty proof sheets[4] in length to censorship and made each state responsible to the Confederation for its observance. Everybody knows about the appointment of fully empowered government agents at the universities, the measures against teachers who were remiss in their duties and against the organizations of academics, and finally, the installation of the Mainz Central Investigating Commission. It deserves to be emphasized, however, that the appointment of an ex-

ceptional court which in the name of the entire Confederation was to pass judgment upon the "conspiracy discovered to exist against the Confederation" was frustrated chiefly by the opposition of Emperor Francis. Francis' determination absolutely to preserve the law (besides, of course, his realization that such a federal court would be incompatible with the jurisdictional and sovereign rights of the individual states), and his aversion to having his own universities investigated were the decisive reasons why the regularly competent courts and laws of the German states were not lost to the nation under the coming acts of persecution and why the Mainz Commission was confined to making investigations and arrests.

A single, glossed-over failure: the plan to intervene against the representative constitutions in Germany, which as late as the Vienna congress had been of little concern even to Metternich, was frustrated by Württemberg, Baden, and Bavaria, who resisted Gentz' interpretation of Article 13 and his crude distinction between estate-type and representative constitutions. By adroit maneuvering the federal diet was induced to accept the Carlsbad Decrees and the nation tricked into believing that this acceptance had come about unanimously.

The spiritual unity of the German people was disrupted by tariff barriers to the intellect as it were; the nation, which possessed no common state, no common army, had achieved a central authority, a center for the detection of intellectual and political agitation that seemed dangerous to the existing legal order. What seems objectionable to us is not that investigations into the existence of revolutionary associations occurred but that these investigations by the Mainz Commission had, in the judgment of its sometime chairman Matthias von Rath, the object

---

[3] The *Landwehr,* literally state guard, was a military reserve in Prussia based on conscription. — Ed.

[4] One proof sheet yielded sixteen pages. — Ed.

"not of seeking the culprit for the crime but the crime for the culprit," and that the Commission was goaded into harsh actions even though it could not, however hard it tried, find the "revolutionary plots emanating from the Tugendbund or their authors and perpetrators," as Metternich demanded it do. It was exactly the same in Prussia, where the political police interfered in the realm of the judiciary. Kamptz struggled with E. T. A. Hoffmann, the fair and nonpolitical judge who realized full well that the Giessen Blacks aimed at a unified German republic but who wanted to safeguard the independence and impartiality of the judiciary; Kamptz the while influenced the conduct of trials and the passing of sentences and introduced the concept of high treason into proceedings against the demagogues. In this sense the devastating judgments of even undoubted conservatives will always remain completely valid: "Not in what the conferences have done," wrote the sensible Friedrich Perthes,[5] a man of deep German awareness, "but in what they have not done lies the evil and the danger. If the decrees really aim at nothing more than what they say, then they will do no damage and will suppress some evil; if, however, they intend something else or something more, then they will not accomplish it. That, on the contrary, in these moments of immeasurable danger, the statesmen of the greatest German governments meet to consider the remedies and do nothing, nothing at all, to satisfy the nation's need for freedom and unity—that is shocking." The fearful bitterness that Goerres put into words filled thousands of people, and Wilhelm von Humboldt spoke from the heart for thousands: "All mere police

activity gradually fails in its purpose; it makes the evil steadily worse at the root and never succeeds in stopping all outbreaks—or even discovering them."

The basic principle of the Confederation itself, the internal independence of the individual states, had been severely damaged. Outwardly, Metternich's success was great. Carlsbad marked the greatest height he reached in his European and German policy in the era after 1815. At Aix-la-Chapelle he had risen to be one of the masters of international politics, but Castlereagh was still more a leader than he. At Carlsbad he was the leader; here he imposed his spirit on Germany and created for Austria a leading role such as this state had never enjoyed under the old Roman-German Empire. At the close of the conferences, after a daily work load of twelve to fifteen hours, he felt like a hounded beast; according to Gentz' testimony, however, he also found himself in a state of exaltation and shared with his journalistic spokesman the opinion that this collection of "antirevolutionary, correct, and peremptory measures" was the most brilliant work of his life after the defeat of Napoleon. "What I have wanted to do since 1813, and the horrible Emperor Alexander has always ruined, I have done because he was not here. I have finally been able to follow my ideas completely and to secure my principles of public law on a foundation of 30 million people— 50 million, if we count all the non-German Austrians. Never has a greater unanimity and acquiescence reigned than in our conferences. The emperor is much mistaken if he doubts that he is emperor of Germany." And he privately characterized the presidential bill in the federal diet as the "first law draft in thirty years that has been composed according to the precepts of reason, justice, and experience, without reservation or adornment,

---

[5] Well-known book dealer in Gotha and friend of many intellectuals.—Ed.

plainly but not dully, with neither mystical nor secret inspiration; these phrases are a great accomplishment, one of the most important of my life."

Actually, impressed by the danger to society, Prussia had voluntarily provided the opening for Austria's interference in her affairs; the Austrian state chancellor had only "needed to strengthen the most active principle in the soul of the Hohenzollern, the inhibiting principle"; Prussia had forgotten her position as an independent great power and had become a client of the Habsburg state. In Austria itself only now did the inexorable pressure finally begin to weigh completely on the people; Prussia now resorted to a most Draconian hunt for demagogues; Boyen, Humboldt, Grolmann, and Beyme fell, to Metternich's immense satisfaction; and the plan of a central representation, after a second short reprieve, was as good as buried. Now for the first time the medium and small states were also rigorously supervised by both leading powers, and executed the Carlsbad Decrees with an intensity that was not even asked of them. Metternich took all the credit himself: "Why must I in particular be the one among so many million people who should think where others do not, act where others do not, and write because others cannot?" He forgot that though he was indeed the most active and intellectually most important of the German ultraconservatives, even he could only be effective because the antirevolutionary ideal he represented was an overwhelming European phenomenon: exemplified by Castlereagh, whom Bignon called the corresponding member of the Holy Alliance, by the Tories as well as by Alexander of Russia and the French enemies of liberalism and Bonapartism, by most German governments and by the greater portion of the peace-loving German populace.

PETER VIERECK (b. 1916) is both a Pulitzer prize winning poet and a historian at Mount Holyoke College, where he is now an Alumnae Foundation Professor. He has written extensively on conservatism both as a scholar and advocate. Although he too considers the Carlsbad Decrees an error, he goes even further than Srbik in sympathizing with Metternich's motives, contending that the targets of repression were not all liberal idealists but included racists and totalitarians. This selection is from an article originally presented as a paper before the American Historical Association in 1950.*

Peter Viereck

Bulwark Against Potential Fascism

"What will our friend Metternich say of this great triumph?" asked Nesselrode, the Russian foreign minister, in 1827. He was commenting on the victory of Navarino Bay, where the Turks were defeated by a treacherous surprise attack; and he answered his own question as follows: "He will repeat his old, tiresome principles; he will talk of right;—*vive la force!* It is might which rules the world nowadays, and I am very glad to find that I and my comrades can leave the regulating of affairs to the admirals. These are men to cut the matter short! Never has there been glory comparable to this moment!"

For one who sees Hitlerism and Stalin-

ism as the logical outgrowth of such *Realpolitik,* Metternich reaches his greatest stature in his calm comment on Nesselrode's gloating: "This," said Metternich, "is how Carnot and Danton, and afterwards their imitators [read: Hitler and Stalin], thought and spoke. They were signally overthrown, however, by the same old and tiresome principles."

These two conflicting quotations sum up the issue between the "old principles" of peace-loving internationalism and the "vive la force!" of nationalistic *Realpolitik.*

"Not by speeches and majority votes are the great questions of the day decided . . . but by blood and iron":—this over-

---

*From Peter Viereck, "New Views on Metternich," *The Review of Politics,* XIII (1951), 211–228. The pages reprinted are 218–223 and 227–228, omitting the original footnotes.

quoted phrase of Bismarck's reflects a political universe incompatible with that reflected by Metternich's remark at the Congress of Laibach: "Is there anything in the world today which can take the place of ink, pens, a conference table with its green cover, and a few greater or smaller bunglers?" Metternich's aristocratic system depended on diplomacy. Democratic liberalism depended on what Bismarck dismissed as "majority votes." Both systems preferred "speeches" to "blood," "conference tables" to "iron." Both sought to internationalize Europe. Both failed because of the civil war between them. The men of words of 1848, both the democrats and the aristocratic diplomats, were replaced by the men of action of 1870, whose "vive la force!" has Balkanized Europe's common international heritage into chaos.

The battle between right and right, as Lord Acton[1] said, is more tragic than the battle between right and wrong. Both Metternich and the liberals of 1848 were right or at least shared the truth between them, for both sought a peaceful, ethical, cosmopolitan Europe. They should have joined their aristocratic and democratic half-truths against the whole-lies of their real enemies: the self-styled "realists" of *Realpolitik,* the racists, the militarists, the war-planning irredentists. Because the conservatives and liberals never joined their halves, these nationalist forebears of fascism could triumph, just as a similar disunity between left and right invites communism and fascism in Europe today.

Ever after the French Revolution of 1789, and again after 1815, middle class internationalism and aristocratic internationalism spent their energies in suc-cessfully undermining each other's claims on Europe's loyalty. Wounding each other fatally in 1848, they created a vacuum of loyalty, which nationalism filled by 1870. Nationalism, scourge of modern times and a leading cause of two world wars, was not so inevitable as commonly believed. It was merely the "lucky third" when the two rival international-isms killed each other.

Many liberals combined international-ism with a liberal idealistic version of nationalism, such as Herder and Mazzini preached. The hope that nationalism would turn out to be liberalism is the opti-mistic Wilsonian error that destroyed liberalism and democracy in most of Europe. The decision of liberals to ally with nationalists is perhaps the most fatal mistake of the whole nineteenth century. In a Europe of overlapping nationalities, a Europe of endless Alsace-Lorraines, Schleswig-Holsteins, Sudetenlands, Polish Corridors, Transylvanias, Macedonias, and Triestes—in such a jigsaw-puzzle Europe, nationalism could in no case have asserted its claims except by unliberal blood-and-iron methods. Right from the start, this contradiction inherently doomed liberal hopes for a peaceful nationalism, even if it had never been provoked into still greater violence by the too rigid opposition of Metternich.

Protest must be registered against the habit of calling every anti-Metternichian a "liberal." Sometimes his opponents were genuine liberals or democrats, who may properly stir our sympathy. But in many important instances his so-called liberal opponents were not only nationalists but militarists, racists, anti-semites, or proto-fascists, like the Slav-hating, war-glorifying Jordan, a leading "1848 liberal," whose oratory influenced the Frankfurt assembly to put nationalism before liberalism in the dispute with Polish liberals

---

[1] Lord John Emmerich Acton, British historian. —Ed.

over Posen. It is noteworthy that, when forced to choose between liberalism and nationalism, most liberals chose the latter and ended up by supporting Bismarck's aggressions through the "National Liberal Party"—not to mention intolerant nationalists and anti-semites like Father Jahn and Richard Wagner, both often called "liberals" because anti-Metternichian. The poet Heine knew better, saying in 1832: "Although I am a Radical in England and a Carbonarist in Italy, I am no Demagogue in Germany for the entirely accidental reason that, with the triumph of the latter, several thousand Jewish heads, and precisely the best ones, would fall."

And did fall; which is why the cosmopolitan, racially unprejudiced Metternich was fighting not only the genuine liberals we sympathize with but also the racist and war-loving ancestors of nazism. In these so-called "liberal" German rebels against Metternich, Heine foresaw in 1834: "demoniac energies, that brutal German joy in battle, the insane Berserker rage, Thor leaping to life with his giant hammer." The Dachau death-camps proved Heine right and justified the prophetic warnings of the internationalist Metternich against the reign of terror to which fanatic nationalism would inevitably lead. "I have a feeling of tenderness," wrote Heine, "for Metternich."

Two points should be made about the so-called "liberal opposition" to Metternich in Germany: (1) basically, as shown in its later support of Bismarck, this opposition was far more often nationalist than liberal, often an intolerant nationalism eager to break the long peace of the Concert of Europe; (2) insofar as his opponents were indeed genuine, tolerant liberals in our western sense, they often tended to be abstract doctrinaires. Metternich tried to be what he called "*tout à*

terre, tout historique" [completely down to earth and historical]. In contrast, they tried to transplant into Germany (or Italy) institutions that, suitable for England because they were originally evolved there, had no historic roots in central Europe. Metternich called parliamentary England the world's "freest country." But against transplanting these free institutions overnight into southern or central Europe, he quoted the familiar arguments of Burke about the need for orderly organic development. Whether true or false, these traditionalist-conservative arguments deserve at least to be pondered seriously by a generation that witnessed the tragic failure of liberal hopes in the Russian Revolution.

The author would like to suggest the following tentative hypothesis towards shaping a unifying New View of Metternich. Since inner contradictions ruled out the chance for a truly liberal nationalism in the long run, perhaps the only two real alternatives were: (1) Metternich, with or without the reforms he advocated to his emperor, and (2) the aggressive German nationalism that threatened all Europe. Probably no free democratic alternative to both of these was possible in Germany during 1815–1848. If there were, the present writer would "prefer" it to the Metternich system. The repressive aspect of the latter's system can be defended negatively as the lesser evil of the two alternatives in this hypothesis. But on questions of personal freedom, it can never be defended as a positive good (except by reactionaries not seriously concerned with freedom in the first place).

The two real alternatives may be further characterized and elaborated. There was Metternich's internationalist Hapsburg monarchy, admittedly old-fashioned, slow-moving, illiberal, with censorship and with stupid, stubborn, authoritarian officials. Yet it prevented suicidal national and economic wars among the Danube people. It had through the centuries kept them within the fold of Western civilization as opposed to Turkish, Mongol, or tsarist rule. It acted as an irreplaceable *buffer* of peace protecting central Europe from the grinding millstones of Pan-German expansion from the west and Pan-Slav expansion from the east. One could call this monarchy a benevolent despotism "tempered" not "by assassination" but by gentlemanly inefficiency. Then there was the intolerant German nationalism of Jahn, Arndt, Jordan, Richard Wagner. This in turn would (and did) have two results: (a) as Heine rightly foresaw, a militarist nationalist dictatorship far harder on civil liberties than Metternich's authoritarian, but not totalitarian, Carlsbad Decrees; (b) war and disunity for all Europe instead of the Congress of Vienna internationalism and peace.

How revolutionary, how dangerous really was this nationalism at the time of the Carlsbad Decrees in 1819? According to the liberal Old View, there was no danger of rebellion, no real conspiracy at all, only a "witch hunt" invented by the Machiavellian Austrian diplomat, with the Kotzebue assassination being an unrepresentative accident, misused by Metternich as a pretext for persecuting liberty. Yet the late Veit Valentin, author of the standard history on 1848 and certainly an opponent of Metternich, conceded in his later book, *The German People,* that there were several real conspiracies for violent revolt as well as the preaching of political murder to university students by the Jena "unconditional" faction, to which Kotzebue's assassin Sand belonged. Significantly this murderer was openly hailed all over Germany as a national

hero by fanatics, some of whom dipped their daggers in his sacred blood. "This group" (says Valentin of Follen's "unconditionals") "wanted to wage political war by means of terrorism—by revolt, murder, and every kind of violence against the established authorities. Though only a small minority, it was very active. Sand's deed was the *result of a conspiracy.* Other conspiracies and an attempted assassination followed."[2]

Although such rebels did try to wage political revolt against the authorities by murder and violence, Metternich's Carlsbad Decrees did not reply by murder and violence; nor did they reply by executions and mass-arrests without trial, in the fashion of today's "police state." Instead these Decrees relied mainly on censorship and on relatively mild surveillance of such dangerous inciters of a German-racist war of conquest as Jahn and his "gymnast" camouflage.

Without justifying the unjustifiable Carlsbad Decrees, one should be ever aware that these measures of Metternich were milksop compared with the racist, anti-semitic, war-plotting dictatorship favored by such influential anti-Metternichian agitators as Jahn. Metternich said his aim in these repressions was to save Germany from "the dictatorship of such men as Jahn and Arndt." Unfortunately Metternich after 1819 went beyond his restraint of this fierce German nationalism. He inexcusably censored academic freedom. Even so, this inquiry accused only 107 rebels in eight years in all Germany.

Since both nationalists and liberals were almost entirely middle class, the broad masses of central Europe were not

---

[2] For Valentin's overall assessment of Metternich, however, see the selection in this volume, pp. 125. —Ed.

involved in this struggle with Metternich or his Emperor. The masses craved, after the wars ended in 1815, the European peace he provided. Metternich's objection to capitalist dictatorship over the masses by middle class nationalists and liberals was not just an insincere slogan. . . .

Psychologically the present beginning of a more favorable view of Metternich is part of an atmosphere where conservatism in general is becoming more useful, more needed, less harmful and stultifying than it often was in the past. In Europe's Victorian era, civilization was stuffy and stodgy: conservatism at its worst. At that time it was healthful—in fact, indispensable—to stir up placid reality and to poke pompous old civilization in the ribs. But today, in the era of terror and total war and atom bombs, today the real Old Fogey is the doctrinaire radical modernist: the dully "daring" bohemian rebel against conservatism. In this chaotic age, when there are few artistic or political traditions left to overthrow, culture is less threatened by conservative conventionality than by the rheumatic jitterbugging[3] of our aging *enfants terribles*. Today the whole world is *terrible*. This means that conservatism and traditionalism, besides giving us some assured values to cling to in the tempest, give a truer and more independent criticism of the age than the maintenance of that fashionable radicalism which merely adds to the tempestuous, *terrible* reality already existing. . . .

---

[3] The wild dance style of Viereck's and my generation.—Ed.

Metternich's greatest mistake, transforming him from an enlightened, peace-making, Burkean conservative into a harmful reactionary, was getting into a panic over the Red Menace of his day: the French Revolution. This proves his relevance, even that of his mistakes, to our own day. For we must never let panic over the Russian Revolution lead to the suppression not merely of our treasonable communist fifth-column but also of non-treasonable independent thinkers with refreshingly unorthodox ideas. Therefore, let us end with a little known and perhaps surprising statement by Metternich about thought control (recorded by Baron Hübner shortly *prior* to Metternich's fall, so that it is not merely wise-after-the-event.) It is a statement Metternich himself should have heeded in 1819 and is just possibly a warning for us of 1951:

[The Emperor Francis] followed my advice in everything on foreign policy. He did not do so in internal affairs. . . . Attributing a perhaps exaggerated importance to the secret societies . . . he thought he found the remedy against the evil in a minute surveillance of the would-be intellectual classes exercised by the police, who thereby became one of the chief instruments of his government; . . . in short, in a moral closing of the frontiers. . . . The result was a dull irritation against the government among the educated classes. I told that to the emperor; but on that point he was unshakable. All I could do to lessen the grievous results, I did. . . . If in 1817, even as late as 1826, the emperor had adopted my ideas on the reorganization of the diets, we would be perhaps in a position to face the tempest. Today it is too late. . . . It is useless to close the gates against ideas; they overleap them. . . .

In this second selection from the work of HENRY A.
KISSINGER we find a certain similarity to the position
of Heinrich von Treitschke. Both see the Carlsbad
Decrees as a function of Austrian power politics. For
Kissinger, however, Metternich's policy was not vile
and arbitrary but reflected real Austrian and (from a
conservative viewpoint) European interests. Notice that
of the four writers in this section he is the only one who
does not specifically say the Decrees were a mistake.*

Henry A. Kissinger

Winner in the Diplomatic
Contest for Germany

. . . By the end of 1818, Metternich had
achieved a stable Central Europe and
Austria was its key. But the rumblings
were not to be stilled, nor was the social
struggle to be avoided simply by exhibit-
ing a monolithic unity. It was expressive
of the feeling of frustration within Germany, and also of the disenchantment
with the Tsar, that the first overt revolutionary act was the assassination of a Russian publicist, who had distinguished
himself by his monarchical writings, and
that it should be carried out by a de-
mented student from the University of
Jena. The assassination of Kotzebue
marked the end of Metternich's effort to
organize Central Europe entirely by political measures. Henceforth he would use
policy primarily as a means to obtain a
moral base for social repression, in a
never-ending quest for the moment of
order which would signal the end of the
revolutionary wave and the survival of
the Central Empire.

Metternich learned of Kotzebue's assassination in Rome, while accompanying
the Emperor on a tour of the Italian
courts. He was informed through a series
of hysterical letters by his associate and
publicist Gentz, who was not free from the
fear that Kotzebue's fate might be in store
for him as well. Gentz urged immediate
repressive steps and Austrian leadership

*From Henry A. Kissinger, *A World Restored: Metternich, Castlereagh, and the Problems of Peace, 1812-1822* (Boston: Houghton Mifflin Company, 1957), pp. 238–246, omitting the original footnotes. Reprinted by permission of the publisher, Houghton Mifflin Company.

of an anti-revolutionary crusade, by-passing the Confederation. But Metternich was too sober to conduct policy in the mood of a moment of hysteria. He saw in Kotzebue's murder not so much a challenge but an opportunity to teach the minor German courts the widom of Austrian homilies. True to his unfailing tactic, he therefore set about to hedge his risks by utilizing the panic in Germany to have Austria offered her objectives by the other courts, to demonstrate Austria's indispensability by a policy of aloofness. For the situation seemed precisely designed to vindicate all of Metternich's preaching over the past three years. Alone of the major German powers, Austria appeared immune to the revolutionary danger. No patriotic societies disturbed the tranquillity of Austrian universities, nor was its press an organ of anti-governmental propaganda. If this was more a tribute to the excellence of Austria's police than to its moral homogeneity, it nevertheless furnished a useful basis from which to operate.

There began again one of Metternich's periods of maddening inactivity, designed to force his potential allies into revealing the extent of their commitment. Metternich was quite prepared to head an anti-revolutionary crusade, but he wanted to be sure to involve the maximum number of other powers, and Prussia above all. He was more than willing to by-pass the Confederation, if only to demonstrate that important problems could be solved better on the basis of pure cabinet diplomacy than by a national organ, however attenuated. He wanted to do this, however, not as an act of Austrian self-will, but by demonstrating the impotence of the Confederation so that the other courts would realize "spontaneously" that Austrian assistance was their only protection. For anyone familiar with Metternich's diplomacy it is not surprising, therefore, that he opened his diplomatic campaign — by doing nothing. He returned a very non-committal reply to Gentz, which in its tone of abstracted indifference was designed to make evident his mastery of the situation. He devoted one paragraph to Kotzebue's murder, which he ascribed to a national conspiracy, and several pages to reflections on the architectual marvels of Rome, and to the relationship between scale, beauty, and spirituality. Gentz, who could barely restrain his hysteria, suggested in reply that the real problem was not to repress a national conspiracy but to reform the system of university education which had produced it, and he enclosed a letter by an Austrian consul in Saxony which blamed the whole turmoil on the Reformation. But, once again his ardour was cooled by Metternich, who was convinced that maximum measures were certain to be advanced in other quarters if Gentz's letters were an even approximate reflection of the spirit among the German powers. He showed his unconcern by leaving for Naples, one stage further removed from the seat of the turmoil, and replied that educational reform should be confined to the system of academic discipline. "As for the Reformation," he wrote acidly, "I cannot deal with Dr. Martin Luther from the Quirinal and I hope that it will prove possible to do some good without uprooting Protestantism at its very core."

In the meantime, the other German governments were becoming panicky. The King of Prussia instituted a commission to investigate revolutionary tendencies and immediately recalled all Prussian students from Jena, an example followed by many other courts. So powerful was this trend that the Grand-Duke of Weimar, who had distinguished himself by his liberalism, but who had the misfortune that the offending university was located in his territory, proposed that the Assembly of the Confederation develop a uniform system of academic discipline for all of Germany. It did not matter that the unfortunate Duke protested his devotion to academic freedom and to his constitution, one more opponent of Metternich had been lured into a precipitate act. If even the liberal Grand-Duke of Weimar admitted the need for the reform of universities, who could blame the Austrian minister for following suit? And if the Assembly proved incapable of dealing with this urgent matter, was not Metternich merely expressing the consensus of Germany if he proposed an alternative procedure? Over the protests of the doctrinaire Gentz, Metternich therefore ordered the Austrian representative to go along with the Grand-Duke's proposal. "There is no point in treating this arch-Jacobin (the Grand-Duke) with contempt," he explained to Gentz. "He is used to that. It seems much wiser to interpret his designs favourably, to trap him on his own ground or to expose him as a liar." It soon became apparent that the Assembly was not the proper organ for decisive action, as Metternich, who had designed it, well knew. While the Grand-Duke's proposal languished in committee, the hysteria of the German governments, which saw assassins lurking everywhere, hardly knew any bounds. With the Confederation discredited and Austrian indispensability sufficiently demonstrated, the moment for action had arrived. "There is no more time to be lost," wrote Metternich now. "Today the governments are afraid enough to act; soon their fear will have reached the stage of paralysis."

On 17 June, more than two months after he had learned of Kotzebue's assassination and while he was finally on the way north,

Metternich transmitted a plan of action to Gentz. He was going to Carlsbad for a rest, and he had arranged for the ministers of the German power to meet him there. His proposals to his colleagues would be based on the axioms that moral dangers could prove more dissolving than physical threats, that the common nationality made the isolation of even the most unimportant German state chimerical, and that only concerted and preventive measures could stem the revolutionary tide. The extent of the danger was sufficiently demonstrated by the fact that conspiracy had found a violent expression in Germany, the one country where it was traditionally confined to the pen. For this he blamed above all the universities and the license of the press. Only a tightened academic discipline and a system of censorship could reverse the trend. Little wonder that Gentz replied jubilantly: "My dark forebodings seem to evaporate when I see the one man in Germany, capable of free and decisive action, scale such heights. . . ."

But Metternich wanted to leave nothing to chance. Although there was no real danger that Prussia would pursue a revolutionary policy, it was by no means certain how far she would go in supporting repressive measures. Nor did Metternich want to be placed in the position of imposing his will on the secondary powers. A repressive programme identified with Austria might strengthen Prussia, the state which so many patriots still considered as the exponent of a national mission. But by the same token, a repressive programme advanced by Prussia would undermine her last remaining advantage: the ability to appeal to the national movement. When Metternich visited the King of Prussia on 28 July at Teplitz, he therefore had two objectives: to develop a common programme for the

Carlsbad conferences in order to separate Prussia from German nationalism; and to keep the King from implementing his promise to grant a constitution in order to paralyse the efforts of certain Prussian statesmen, such as Humboldt, to ally Prussia with German liberalism.

There ensued a strange and wonderful dialogue between Metternich and the Prussian king, in which Metternich, like a stern teacher, remonstrated about Prussia's sins, while the King, thoroughly chastened, desperately attempted to shift the blame on to his own ministers. For to the panicky King, Metternich appeared on the scene as a prophet and a saviour. Had he not warned innumerable times, not least at Aix-la-Chapelle, against the dangers of a constitution? Had he not predicted the revolutionary danger? "Everything you foresaw has occurred," said the crestfallen King. But Metternich was severe. The revolution, he asserted, had merely been the demonstration which always follows the lesson. Its origin had been in Prussia, while Austria itself remained unaffected. Nevertheless, animated by its policy of friendship, Austria was willing to assist in stemming the revolutionary tide, but it would first have to determine which governments deserved that name. Should they be found wanting and indecisive, Austria would simply withdraw into its shell. Terrified by the prospect of being left alone in Germany with the Revolution, the King now blamed the associates of his Chancellor Hardenberg. In order to rectify his errors, and to demonstrate his good intentions, he suggested that Metternich, the minister of the power which had most to lose from a national policy, advise Hardenberg, the Chancellor of the state which had most to gain from it, on the constitutional structure suitable for Prussia. Metternich replied with a memorandum which explained that the promise of an assembly in Article XIII of the Act of Confederation did not necessarily imply representative institutions and to this, too, the Prussian King agreed. What could better illustrate Metternich's dominance than the King's plaintive advice as Metternich prepared to negotiate with the Prussian ministers: "Try, above all, to commit these people [the Prussian ministers] in writing"? Well might Metternich report triumphantly to his Emperor: "I found two negative elements engaged in a contest: the weakness of the King with the impotence of the Chancellor. . . . I conceived it my task so to strengthen the most active element in the King's soul, that tending towards paralysis, that he will hardly dare to take the boldest of all steps, that of introducing a constitution."

The result was the Convention of Teplitz by which Austria and Prussia agreed on a common programme. Two conferences were to be held: in Carlsbad and in Vienna. The Carlsbad conference would deal with the immediate dangers and consider steps to restrain freedom of the press, to regulate the universities and to establish a Central Commission to investigate the revolutionary movement. The conference in Vienna would deal with the organic institutions of the Confederation, particularly the interpretation of Article XIII. In addition, Hardenberg promised that no constitution would be introduced in Prussia until complete order was restored and then only with assemblies in the "literal," that is the Metternich, sense of deputations of provincial Estates. In short, Austria's domestic legitimization had become the organizing principle of Germany.

With the ground thus carefully prepared the result of the Carlsbad Conference, which opened on 6 August, could not be in doubt. Its tone was set by the representative of Nassau, who expressed his warmest gratitude to Austria which "itself unaffected by the revolutionary current, has conceived the measures to arrest it." The Austro-Prussian proposals were accepted in their entirety. Each state undertook to submit publications of less than twenty pages to censorship and to suppress those found objectionable by any member of the Confederation. Thus every state, and Austria above all, had a complete veto over all publications within the territory of the Confederation. The universities were placed under the supervision of the governments by appointing a representative in each, charged with enforcing discipline and surveilling the spirit of the lectures. And a Central Commission with Headquarters in Mainz was to investigate revolutionary activities. So strong was Metternich's position that he could afford to appear as the advocate of moderation. It was Prussia which insisted on setting the number of pages [proof sheets] subject to censorship at twenty, while Metternich would have been satisfied with fifteen. And when Prussia proposed the establishment of a special court not only to investigate but to try revolutionaries, Metternich insisted on the impossibility of trying individuals on the basis of ex-post-facto laws.

Metternich had succeeded in a *tour de force:* Austria, the most vulnerable state, appeared as the repository of strength; the power which had most to gain from the Carlsbad decrees emerged as the most disinterested party. The deferential address with which the assembled diplomats thanked Metternich for having been permitted to do his bidding showed that conquest need not always take the form of arms: "If we may hope that this task, as difficult as it is honourable, for which you

have assembled us, has been concluded in a manner not unacceptable to you, then we owe it to your . . . wise leadership. . . . When, while still on the other side of the Alps, you heard the clamour of undisciplined scribes and the news of a monstrous crime, . . . you recognized the real cause of the evil . . . and that which we have accomplished here is no more than what you already conceived then." The opprobrium heaped by posterity on Metternich's self-satisfied letters overlooked that much of the time they merely reflected the reality of extraordinary situations. So this missive from Carlsbad: "For the first time [in thirty years] there will appear a group of measures, anti-revolutionary, correct and peremptory. That which I have wanted to do since 1813 and which this terrible Emperor Alexander has always spoiled, I have accomplished now, because he was not present. . . . If the Emperor of Austria doubts that he is Emperor of Germany, he is mistaken." It was a paradoxical situation, dear to the whimsical streak in Metternich, that by giving up the Imperial Crown, Franz had become Emperor of Germany.

In this manner the Carlsbad Conferences ended with a spontaneous affirmation of Austrian predominance. Metternich was in effect the Prime Minister of Germany while protesting his disinterest. Prussia, with its own eager acquiescence, was diverted into a direction which kept it for over a generation from identifying itself with the national current; its more liberal ministers, such as Humboldt, were soon forced from office. And the German Confederation was reduced to a meeting place of subsidiary diplomats, while the really fundamental decisions were taken by direct negotiations among the Cabinets. The only organ which represented all of Germany had become a ratifying instrument. On 20 September, it approved unanimously and without debate the decisions taken at Carlsbad. So ended, for the time being, the dream of a unified Germany.

But Metternich's victory was not complete if what he called the revolutionary movement obtained foreign support. Should the foreign powers refuse to sanction the Carlsbad decrees, Austria would be put on the defensive not only within Germany but all over Europe. And as the Vienna conferences approached, the South German courts, particularly Württemberg, were becoming restive under the Austro-Prussian tutelage. Metternich, therefore, invited Britain and Russia to approve the Carlsbad decrees. But this only brought to a head the difficulty of Castlereagh's position. It was impossible for any British statesman to express approval of a policy of domestic repression, however much he might sympathize with it. Nor could he countenance what was in effect a doctrine of general interference in the domestic affairs of other states. Despite his personal good will, Castlereagh had to confine himself to this reply to the Austrian ambassador: "We are always glad to see evil germs destroyed without the power to give our approval openly."

Russia proved even more difficult. Capo d'Istria represented to the Tsar the danger of Austrian domination of Germany and did not fail to point out that the chief opponent of Alexander's *Alliance Solidaire* was now applying its maxims to his own advantage. The result was a Russian circular-note, testy and non-committal, which stated that if the Carlsbad decrees concerned German matters, Russia was not entitled to interfere, while if it was a European affair, Russia should have been invited to Carlsbad. On 4 December, Capo d'Istria even sounded out Castlereagh regarding the possibility of a joint representation to the Vienna conference.

But if Castlereagh was unable to sanction Metternich's policy, he could at least prevent the Tsar from using it as an excuse to exploit the difficulties of Central Europe for Russian ends. If the principle of non-interference was a doctrine of self-limitation for Britain, it could also be used as a shield behind which Metternich could organize Central Europe. Castlereagh therefore returned a very skilful reply to the Russian proposition. He admitted that the Acts of the Confederation were part of the Vienna settlement, and that foreign powers had the right to protest against their violation. But he denied that the Carlsbad decrees were anything other than a legitimate effort to insure domestic tranquillity, a goal he was certain Russia approved. Britain had not officially replied to the notification of the Carlsbad decrees, precisely because to give an opinion would have been to interfere in the domestic affairs of Germany. At the same time, Castlereagh sent a dispatch to his ambassador in Berlin making clear that Britain could do no more and that the German powers should not prolong the dispute: "Our Allies must recollect that we have a Parliament to meet and it is essential . . . not to have angry discussions on continental politics. . . ."

The Carlsbad decrees marked the turning-point in European politics, the marginal case of Austro-British co-operation, the border-line where the doctrine of non-interference could be used to localize a social struggle. Because Austria was strong enough to defeat the revolution within Germany without the aid of non-German powers, the difference between

Castlereagh and Metternich could still be obscured by utilizing *political* weapons to frustrate Russian intervention. On negative measures, on creating a framework of inaction, Metternich and Castlereagh were still agreed. But it was obvious that as soon as the social struggle took on a wider scope, a doctrine of inaction would not satisfy Metternich. Just as he had involved Prussia in his German policy, he was certain to attempt to involve Russia in his European efforts. This became all the more important as the experience of the Carlsbad decrees had shown that Russian approval might not be obtainable retroactively. The crucial test of Allied unity must come when the contest became explicitly social and on a European scale. And as the year 1820 progressed, revolutions breaking out in the most different parts of Europe announced that Alliances, no more than human beings, can live on the memory of the past and that the meaning of unity would have to be redefined in the light of the present.

A. J. P. TAYLOR (b. 1906), a Fellow at Magdalen
College, Oxford, and Librarian of the Beaverbrook
Library, is the author of many books on European
history, most of them on diplomacy and all of them to
some degree controversial. In fact, he has sometimes
quarreled with himself, as witness his book on the
Habsburg monarchy. The first edition, published
during World War II (1941), contained a strong liberal
animus against Austria's rulers; the completely
rewritten version of 1948, from which this excerpt is
taken, is much more sympathetic. In the passages that
follow, Metternich is presented as a man who
understood Austria's problems even if he was not up to
devising or carrying out adequate solutions.*

A. J. P. Taylor

Perceptive But Superficial Tinkerer

Habsburg creativeness had had a last
explosion with Joseph II. Francis, bat-
tered in youth by his uncle Joseph and in
manhood by his son-in-law Napoleon,
had been hammered into obstinate negation. His only quality was a stubbornness
in resisting foreign enemies and domestic
change. Mediocre in character and intelligence, he would have made a tolerable
Tsar, ruler of a ramshackle empire where
most things ran on without direction from
above. But Austria was not Russia: it was
a centralised state, with a more developed
and extensive bureaucracy than any other
in Europe. Thanks to Maria Theresa and
Joseph II, the Emperor of Austria could
really govern: he could make his will
felt throughout the Empire. Francis had
no will and left the bureaucrats without
direction or policy. The defects of this
system are not so startling to the modern
observer as they were to contemporaries,
with their smaller experience of bureaucratic rule. The Austrian bureaucracy
was fairly honest, quite hard-working,
and generally high-minded; it probably
did more good than harm. It was also slow,
manufactured mountains of paper, regarded the creation of new bureaucratic
posts as its principal object, forgot that it
dealt with human beings; these qualities
are now familiar to the inhabitant of any
civilised state. Still, Austrian bureaucracy
was perhaps more than usually lacking in
policy; and the defect was the more obvious since most of the Austrian bureaucrats

were able and clear-sighted. Hartig, one of Metternich's closest colleagues, expressed the general view: "Administration has taken the place of government."

Organs of government existed, but Francis could not be persuaded to use them. He abolished, revived, and again abolished the Council of State, which had conceived the reforms of Maria Theresa; he established instead a Conference of Ministers, but failed to summon it. Some bureaucrats still carried on the reforming work of Joseph II; others regarded resistance to "Jacobinism" as their sole duty. Some continued the sapping of provincial and aristocratic privileges which had been begun by Maria Theresa; others regarded the provinces and the nobility as the buttresses of the Empire. Some still thought, as Joseph II had done, that the Empire should be based on rationalist philosophy; others wished to call on the police services of the Roman Church. The greatest bureaucratic zeal went into the struggle against "dangerous thoughts." The Empire of Francis I was the classic example of the police state. There was an official, lifeless press; correspondence, even the correspondence of the Imperial family, was controlled; a passport was needed to travel from one province to another or from a town into the country. Yet, like the rest of the system, the censorship was a nuisance rather than a tyranny. Though foreign books and papers were forbidden, the educated classes knew what was astir in the world, and, long before 1848, there was a clear radical programme, not on paper, but in men's minds.

The bureaucratic machine was most successful in a sphere where it was most out of touch with contemporary feeling. Austria was the last surviving example of a planned mercantilist economy; in this, more than in anything else, it challenged liberal doctrine. Hungary, with its separate tariff and its separate system of taxation, lay outside this economy and remained almost exclusively agricultural until after 1848; in the rest of the Empire industrial development was still promoted from above. Old Austria, before its death, left two legacies to central Europe, neither of which could have been produced by *laissez-faire:* the Austrian railway system and the port of Trieste.[1] Austria was ahead of Prussia in railway development and began, in the Semmering line, the first railway in Europe through mountainous country. Trieste, a project inconceivable before the age of railways, was deliberately built up by Imperial initiative to give central Europe an outlet to the Mediterranean and so to escape dependence on the Danube. Even in Lombardy-Venetia, Austrian rule brought economic benefits. Taxes and military service were lighter than previously under Napoleon or than they were afterwards in national Italy; and, as well, Austrian officials were honest—a unique experience for the Italians. Still, these achievements counted for nothing in the balance of politics. Austrian rule often benefited the peasant masses, but these were dumb; it offended the liberal sentiment of the educated middle classes, and these determined the political atmosphere of the time.

Many of the bureaucrats desired to win wider favour, though without weakening their system; Metternich was the most fertile, though not the most energetic, of these reformers. In 1821 he was given the title of Chancellor, as reward for his successful diplomacy; and this position gave him some claim to act as general adviser to the Emperor. Besides, he was quick, superficially clever, and with great experience of the world; and, though him-

---

[1] This is the Italian version. Correct name: Trst.

self incapable of constructing a general system of politics, had in his assistant Gentz the ablest political writer of the age. Francis disliked change when it was proposed by Metternich as much as when it was proposed by anyone else; and none of Metternich's projects was applied. Metternich lacked that driving force to translate ideas into action which is the mark of the great statesman; and Habsburg circumstances were such that, if he had possessed it, he would only have driven himself out of public life. He was a professor in politics; and his schemes, intellectually adroit, guessed at all the devices by which later professors hoped to solve, that is to evade, the "Austrian problem." That problem was, in essence, simple: the Habsburg Monarchy and nationalism were incompatible, no real peace was possible between them.

Metternich saw this more clearly than many of his successors, certainly more clearly than the well-meaning theorists of the early twentieth century who attributed the failure of the Habsburg Monarchy to some imagined "lost opportunity." Metternich explored, too, all the remedies, and despaired of them. He tried repression and associated his name for ever with the horrors of the Spielberg.[2] This repression was halfhearted: it could not have been other without the Monarchy losing the civilised character which it genuinely possessed. Metternich practised also the method of the "Austrian mission": economic amelioration which would make the masses grateful for Habsburg rule. The mission was genuine, the result disastrous; every advance in prosperity increased the national problem, at first of the Germans, later of the other peoples. An economic programme,

to achieve its effect, would have had to appeal to the masses, not to offer middle-class prosperity; the Habsburgs would have had to become Communists, as Metternich was accused of being in Galicia in 1846 and as Bach was accused after 1848. Perhaps this is what Metternich meant by wishing that he had been born a century later. As it was, he was forced back on constitutional concessions, or rather deceptions: these were to appease discontent without lessening the Emperor's power. In the words of his biographer, they offered to a hungry man pictures of still life. Francis Joseph had, later, the same aim; hence Metternich's suggestions anticipated all the constitutional developments of Austria in the second half of the nineteenth century. The composition and very name of the central Parliament; the composition of the provincial Diets; and the relations between Parliament and Diets were all first sketched in Metternich's useless memoranda, which lay disregarded in a drawer of the Emperor's desk. Metternich was the ablest man who ever applied himself to the "Austrian problem"; the practical effect of his actions was least. Understanding best the Habsburg Monarchy, he despaired of it soonest.

Austria was suffering from a centralised system of government which lacked direction. Metternich's proposals offered two distinct, indeed rival, remedies: to give the centralised system direction and to make it less centralised. Metternich had seen a centralised system working successfully in the Napoleonic Empire, and in all his schemes sought to capture the secret of Napoleon's success. This secret was simple: to have a man of genius as Emperor. This was not a secret which could be commended to Francis nor even admitted by Metternich; and therefore a false solution had to be found in Napo-

---

[2] Fortress and political prison in present-day Brno, Czechoslovakia. — Ed.

leon's Council of State which supposedly laid down the broad principles of Imperial government. Metternich urged a Reichsrat, or Imperial Council, on Francis for more than twenty years. The Reichsrat, Metternich explained, was not to encroach on the Emperor's power, but to formalise it: it was to be "the expression of the legislative power of the monarch." His real intention was revealed when he described it as "restraining the ruler from outbursts of momentary impulse." Francis preferred to have no restraint and disregarded the scheme; no man relinquishes power without being forced to do so. Still, the name of Reichsrat had been put into circulation; and it was as the Reichsrat that the Austrian Parliament met until 1918. Metternich had puzzled, too, over the composition of his projected Council. He recognised that it would not improve the bureaucratic system, if it were merely composed of bureaucrats; and he proposed to bring in new blood. Some of this was merely old blood: retired bureaucrats were to criticise their successors. Some was Imperial blood: the archdukes were to contribute their wisdom, a suggestion particularly unwelcome to Francis, who disliked all his relatives except the half-witted. The real innovation in Metternich's scheme was the proposal that the provincial Diets should send delegates to the Reichsrat, which would thus become, though in strictly advisory capacity, an Estates General of the Empire. Here too Metternich's influence survived: the Reichsrat was elected by the Diets from 1861 until 1873 and on a class system of "estates" until 1907.

Still, the Austrian Parliament would have developed even without these echoes of Metternich's project. His influence had a more special significance in the other part of his proposals—the revival of provincial autonomy. Respect for the provinces was the kernel of the conservatism which Metternich learnt from Gentz, and this romantic anti-Jacobinism revived the decaying provinces to the confusion of later times. Monarchy and conservatism were not historic allies, in the Habsburg Empire least of all. The Habsburg rulers had been the destroyers of historical institutions since the battle of the White Mountian; and Joseph II had given the existing Empire a Jacobinical pattern. Traditional institutions survived in those countries where monarchy failed, in England and the United Provinces; not in countries where monarchy succeeded. The great storm of the French Revolution forced old enemies together: aristocracies, who had been ceaselessly in revolt against their kings, developed grotesque loyalty; kings grew romantic over the traditions which they had done their best to destroy. In France Charles X lost his throne by attempting to restore to the Church and to the nobility the privileges of which they had been deprived by his ancestors; in Prussia Frederick William IV tried to revive the Provincial patriotism which had been the weakness of Prussia; and even in England the epigones of Pitt defended the abuses which Pitt had hoped to reform. Everywhere monarchy was treated as a sentiment rather than as a force; and kings hoped to save themselves from Jacobinism by a "historical" camouflage. They collected traditions as geologists collect fossils, and tried to make out that these fossils were alive.

The greatest enthusiasm for these historical fossils came not from those who had grown up among them, but from strangers, converts simulating respect for alien traditions. Historical awe for the Austrian provinces and their Diets was the invention of Metternich, a Rhinelander, and of Gentz, a Prussian. The

Diets in fact possessed neither power nor significance: they were showy assemblies of the artificial Habsburg nobility, solemnly "examining"—without power of rejection—the laws and proposed taxes that were put before them. Metternich did not propose to give the Diets any power or to make them more representative: he merely wished the historical charades to be played more widely and more often. The Diets were therefore called more regularly and revived in the provinces where they had lapsed; they remained decorative. Yet this political antiquarianism made a deep mark in Austria's history. The moribund provinces became the old bottles into which the new wine of nationalism was poured. Metternich thought that by reviving the provinces he was preparing a "historical" federalism which would strengthen the Empire; actually the provinces became battlegrounds of national ambition and a decisive bar against co-operation between the nationalities. Manufactured traditions were the ruin of Austria; and Metternich was the founder of this trade.

His adventurous, speculative spirit, intellectually convinced of conservatism yet without genuine background, led Metternich along another line of experiment, in contradiction with his policy towards revival of the provinces, though springing from it. Delving in provincial antiquities, Metternich made an unexpected discovery: many of the provinces were not originally German in character. Historical revivalism would thus have the further advantage of weakening the danger from German nationalism. Metternich patronised the Czech literary revival, with its strong historical bent. This could be reconciled with the historic unit of Bohemia. More surprisingly, he welcomed the unhistorical movement for a single South Slav language, an intellec-

tual conception which had its origin in Napoleonic Illyria and was in implication as revolutionary as the idea of national Italy. The main attraction of "Illyrian" was its providing weapons against Hungarian demands, weapons of which the Habsburgs could never have too many. And, no doubt, Metternich, a western German, ignorant of Slav affairs, supposed the Illyrian language could be entangled with Croat history, as the Czech revival overlapped with historic Bohemia. In any case, these literary activities were not meant to have any practical political outcome; they were "cultural nationalism," a substitute for freedom much favoured by absolute rulers. All the same Metternich, by promoting Illyrianism and subsidising the poet Gaj[3] who popularised it, was unconsciously acting against the decaying historic provinces and in favour of national reconstruction. Indeed, Metternich, without realising what he was doing, actually proposed to divide the Empire on national lines. One of his abortive reforms was a proposal to divide the centralised Chancellery into four departments: Austria, Italy, Illyria, and Bohemia-Moravia-Galicia. The first three of these were national groupings, since "Austria" means the Germanic lands; and even the fourth was meant to be national, since it followed the Illyrian analogy and associated Czechs and Poles as "Western Slavs." With the existing Hungarian and Transylvanian Chancelleries, there would thus have been six national units, each using its own language. Except on the one point of Galicia, Metternich in these schemes anticipated all future plans for reconstructing the Habsburg Monarchy; and like the future plans, his, too, were futile, never put into operation. The destinies of cen-

---

[3] Pronounced: Guy.

tral Europe, in Metternich's time and since, were made by the conflict of classes and institutions, not by clever ideas.

The difference between paper schemes and real politics, between simulated conservatism and the genuine article, was shown in Hungary, the only province with a living history. Francis regarded Hungary with traditional Habsburg distrust. Much as he had disliked his uncle Joseph II, he disliked Hungarian resistance to Joseph II still more; and he, too, meant to end Hungary's privileges. This had been impossible during the French wars. The Diet had had to be called in order to secure grants of men and money; and in 1809 Francis had had to pose as a Hungarian patriot in order to counter Napoleon's appeal for a Hungarian revolt. In 1811 Francis sought to equate Hungarian and Imperial currency by depreciating Hungarian currency to the Vienna level; the Diet rejected his demand, and he dissolved it in anger, resolving never to call another. The constitutional provision to summon the Diet every three years was again broken; but, unlike Joseph II, Francis did not also abolish the autonomous administration of the county meetings. To govern Hungary with middle-class German officials demanded a reforming enthusiasm abhorrent to Francis. Deadlock followed. The county committees evaded the orders which they received from the Hungarian Chancellery in Vienna and refused to levy taxes or soldiers without an act of the Diet; they impeded the royal commissioners who were sent in sporadically to undertake the collection of money and levying of men, and in 1823—peak of resistance—the county of Bács[4] actually dismissed all its officials in order to make the work of the commissioners impossible.

---

[4] Pronounced: Batch.

Metternich had always regretted this conflict with the "historic" element; and, vain of his diplomatic skill, he assured Francis that he could manage the Hungarian Diet. It was summoned in 1825, a victory of Hungarian separatism over Habsburg centralism.

Metternich supposed that the Hungarian nobility would be content with a Diet on the level of the other artificial Diets, a historical farce with Metternich playing the chief role. The promoters of the Imperial cause in Hungary were the Germans, urban traders originally introduced into Hungary by the Monarchy of deliberate purpose. These might have been won to Metternich's side by a programme of fiscal and franchise reform: ending the nobles' exemption from taxation and increasing the representation of the towns. But this would have been "liberalism" and, as well, an association with German nationalism: Metternich preferred to patronise historic Hungary, as he patronised historic Bohemia. The great aristocracy in Hungary, too, saw the menace of liberalism and of nationalism; but instead of seeking Habsburg protection, they found safety by putting themselves at the head of the national movement and so won the support both of the lesser nobility and of the German town-dwellers. The pioneer of this change was Széchényi, a great landowner, who had penetrated the secret of Whig success in England; in a gesture which founded modern Hungary, he offered a year's income from his estates to found a Hungarian Academy. The great aristocracy became patriotic; and, at the same time, patriotism became national. The first demands for the "national" tongue, Magyar, instead of Latin were made in 1825; they were made still more insistently in the Diet of 1830. Hungary had previously been distinguished from the rest of the Empire only by her antiquated privileges; henceforward she appeared as a distinct national state.

The Hungarian Diets of 1825 and 1830 belied Metternich's cleverness and weakened his influence with the Emperor. Metternich was shaken, too, by the increasing confusion of the Austrian finances. He had been engaged to promote peace. Instead, he contemplated war with Russia in 1829 and had to call for mobilisation in 1830, during the alarm which followed the July Revolution in France; these were expensive steps. Success in finance was the making of Metternich's rival Kolovrat, a Bohemian aristocrat who had been called to the central government in 1826. Kolovrat had none of Metternich's highflying conservatism; he was a bureaucrat in the tradition of Joseph II, jealous of the provinces and contemptuous of tradition. His main motive was personal — dislike of the "foreigner" Metternich and of his expenditure of Austrian strength in European schemes. Playing at opposition to Metternich, he posed sometimes as a liberal, sometimes as a Bohemian patriot. Of great private wealth, he constantly used the weapon of threatened resignation to get his way; and Metternich, chained to office by his need for money, was helpless against him. In 1831 Kolovrat balanced Austria's accounts, a unique event in the reign of Francis; henceforth he was secure in the Emperor's favour. Francis had no personal liking for Kolovrat and he got on well with Metternich; but Kolovrat enabled him to disregard Metternich's criticism of the system of government. Domestic affairs, and especially the appointment of officials, became the sphere of Kolovrat; Metternich was confined to the direction of foreign policy.

In 1832 Metternich once more tried his political skill in Hungary. He recognised now that the Diet could not be satisfied with decorative functions and hoped to divert it by a programme of practical reform, modernising the confusion of Hungarian law. The Hungarian nobility, trained for generations in county meetings, understood the realities of politics and resisted this programme of reform from above. The lower house was kept from open defiance of royal authority only by the exertions of the magnates, and no reforms were accomplished. Against this failure, Metternich could set foreign success: the agreement with Russia in 1833. His standing with Francis began once more to rise; and at the beginning of 1835, Francis promised to create the Imperial Council which Metternich had so often advocated. This promise, too, was not fulfilled. Francis died in February, 1835. On his deathbed he put his signature to two political testaments to his son, which Metternich had drafted long before. One laid on Ferdinand the duty of freeing the Church from the control which Joseph II had imposed upon it; the other enjoined him not to alter anything in the bases of the state, to consult Archduke Lewis (the youngest brother of Francis) in all internal affairs, and, above all, to rely on Metternich, "my most loyal servant and friend." Kolovrat was not mentioned. It seemed that Metternich was at last free of his rival and could carry out the programme of constructive conservatism which he had long advocated. Returning to the Chancellery, he announced the death of Francis to his physician with the words: "Ferdinand is Emperor." The doctor, simpleton or sycophant, replied: "And you are Richelieu."

With the death of Francis began the interregnum of "pre-March," the strange period of waiting which everyone was conscious would end in the "deluge." The new Emperor Ferdinand was an imbecile, epileptic and rickety; his character was expressed in his only sensible remark, "I'm the Emperor and I want dumplings!"[5] Metternich had foreseen the evils of an Empire without an Emperor, yet he had strengthened Francis's unwillingness to change the succession. There was no attractive alternative: Francis Charles, the younger brother, though not actually half-witted, was almost as ill-fitted to rule, and besides, Metternich argued, to alter the succession would shake the principle of hereditary monarchy. Metternich's real motive was more practical, a true diplomat's trick: with an emperor incapable of governing, Metternich would become the real ruler of the Habsburg Monarchy and at last carry out his programme of conservative reform. Yet he lacked the self-confidence of Richelieu or Bismarck and, even now, had to shelter behind an archduke; he supposed that he had made himself safe by choosing Archduke Lewis, the most insignificant of Francis's brothers. The House of Habsburg had two able members, Archduke Charles, a great military organiser, and Archduke John, a convinced liberal; but both had sought reform by criticising Metternich and therefore they remained excluded from power.

The nomination of Lewis was the stroke of a diplomat, not of a statesman; for if Metternich were really to reform the Monarchy he needed the support of a strong, resolute man, not of a nonentity. Metternich did not understand the realities of the political situation: he genuinely supposed that the only defect was in the character of the Emperor and allowed neither for the dead-weight of bureaucracy nor for the jealousy of the true-born

Austrians against his clever "foreign" schemes. In fact, the success of Metternich's intrigue made Kolovrat the leader of a patriotic Austrian resistance in court circles. At first Kolovrat ignored the way in which he had been passed over. The conflict broke out in 1836. Metternich had already perceived the danger to Austria's German position in the Zollverein[6], which had been founded under Prussian leadership in 1834, and he intended to change the Austrian tariff, so as to make Asutrian inclusion in the Zollverein possible. As a beginning he proposed in 1836 a reduction in the sugar duties, a blow against the great estates, which had already discovered the profitable crop of sugar-beet. Kolovrat protested and, withdrawing to his Bohemian estate, threatened to resign. This was Metternich's opportunity. He proposed to Lewis the creation of a Reichsrat, or sham-parliament, and a Conference of Ministers, or sham-cabinet, both under the chairmanship of Metternich — constitutional bodies without representative character, a true conservative's dream. Lewis, glad enough to be free of responsibility, agreed.

These were paper schemes, without solid backing from any class or party; made by one court intrigue, they could be undone by another. The defeat of Metternich was initiated, with deserved symbolism, by Archduke John, the liberal Habsburg. During the Napoleonic Wars John had wanted Austria to lead German national resistance, and he had patronised the Tyrolese revolt against the Bavarian rule imposed by Napoleon; these activities had endangered Metternich's diplomacy of delay and had brought the disapproval of Francis. John, who had

---

[5] Strictly he demanded noodles. But for a noodle to ask for noodles would be in English an intolerable pun.

[6] German customs union joined by most German states but not Austria. — Ed.

completed his liberalism by marrying a postmaster's daughter, had been exiled from court for a generation. He knew Metternich only as a reactionary and as a friend of the obscurantist Church, and supposed that Metternich's coup marked the victory of his reactionary policy. He came to court for the first time in twenty-five years and urged on Lewis the disastrous effects of adopting Metternich's plans; coached by the aristocrats who feared for their sugar-beet profits, he praised Kolovrat as a successful financier and as a liberal spirit. Metternich had no force behind him; his only weapon was argument, but three hours and a half of argument failed to shake John's opposition. Lewis, badgered and bewildered, withdrew his approval; scrapped the Reichsrat; and decided that he himself would preside at the Conference of Ministers, which became again a formality as it had been in the reign of Francis. Kolovrat returned in triumph to his bureaucratic desk.

Metternich's diplomacy, successful in negation, had failed in constructing. Nothing had changed; or rather things changed for the worse. The Imperial power was put in commission: a "pre-conference" of Lewis, Metternich, and Kolovrat decided on the business which should be passed on to the ministers. This pre-conference did the work of the ministers over again, as Francis had done, and with even greater delay. Kolovrat and Metternich hated each other, and Lewis hated activity of any kind. There was therefore always a majority against action; the stoppage was complete. Not only had administration taken the place of government; even the administration was not working.

Metternich had failed to reform the central government; his attempts to revive provincial sentiment had more results in "pre-March," though not the results which he intended. Oddly enough, Metternich and Kolovrat bid against each other for provincial favour, especially in Bohemia: Kolovrat, though a "Josephine" centralist, disliked the Germans and paraded Bohemian patriotism; Metternich, though a German, disliked centralisation. Traditional provincial ceremonies were revived. Ferdinand had been crowned King of Hungary in 1830, during his father's lifetime; he was crowned King of Bohemia in 1836 and received the iron crown of Lombardy in 1838—futile masquerade of Austrian Italy. Metternich wished to invent a new pseudo-historical rigmarole and to have Ferdinand crowned Emperor of Austria in the presence of delegates from the provincial Diets; this was a manufacture of tradition too artificial even for pre-March Austria.

In the preceding selection Taylor makes light of Metternich's plans to decentralize the monarchy, questioning his understanding of nationalism and ridiculing the provincial diets which the minister hoped to resuscitate. The American scholar ARTHUR G. HAAS (b. 1925), on the other hand, argues that Metternich's plans were imaginative, constructive, and even realistic in that there was still a chance of reconciling what he calls "national feeling" with the interests of the dynasty. Haas, now professor of history at the University of Tennessee, studied this problem for many years as a fellow at the Institute for European History at Mainz, Germany, and in the Vienna archives. The passages reproduced here are based on painstaking, exhaustive research in the original documents.*

Arthur G. Haas

Enlightened But Thwarted Reformer

To harmonize the apparently contradictory principles of unity and diversity had always been a primary problem accompanying the integration of the Habsburg lands. Yet, this very prudent harmonization—so often stressed by Metternich—called for a careful balancing of institutions which, however, was seldom attained. Usually, during the many phases of Habsburg history, dynastic and state policy inclined toward one or the other of these principles. Until the reign of Joseph II, a tendency to respect heterogeneity prevailed. The very manner in which various territories, often historic entities, had come into the Habsburg collection of states usually required a maintenance of special status and accepted custom. This seemed the only feasible way to avoid either the risk of offending local estates or the unwelcome task of providing a new administration. Generally, heterogeneity and territorial chancelleries—such as for Transylvania, the Banat, or Illyria—were even encouraged to check what were felt to be excessive Hungarian pretensions. Conversely, the idea of special status and diversity ran counter to rationalistic and centralistic concepts of state which guided "enlightened" rulers in the modernizing of their governing apparatus. . . .

*From Arthur G. Haas, *Metternich, Reorganization and Nationality, 1813–1818. A Story of Foresight and Frustration in the Rebuilding of the Austrian Empire* (Wiesbaden: Franz Steiner Verlag GMBH, 1963 [American Edition, Knoxville: University of Tennessee Press, 1964]), pp. 118–119, 150–151, 45, 112, 99–100, 112, 147–148, 152, omitting the original footnotes. This work is distributed in the United States by The University of Tennessee Press, Knoxville.

During the Wars of Liberation, various European powers had learned to fight the French with some of their own weapons; one of these had been the appeal to national spirit and the promise of national independence to various subject nationalities. That such appeals and promises were frequently phrased and interpreted to imply more than just freedom from French domination drew no objections until it became clear that such methods might be incongruous with political aims. In such areas as Northern Italy and Illyria, new control and a political program did not follow the French collapse firmly or quickly enough. This situation forceful men immediately exploited in order to assert independence or to demand satisfaction of national interests. Soon, however, the hard truth that Austria's intentions or power could not be prevailed against reduced manifestations of nationalism to more modest entreaties for national autonomy. Fortunately for Austria, such manifestations of national feeling were more regional than national in their extent—a fact which Metternich recognized and sought to turn to Austria's advantage by encouraging regional *esprit*. In this manner Austria came upon the need to reconcile several national groups to a rather dubious political fortune by demonstrating that membership in the Habsburg "family of nations" would be worthwhile.

Metternich realized that the unique opportunity to reorganize in Europe applied particularly to the Habsburg empire. First, however, came the practical problems arising from the reincorporation of lost or new territories. He knew that in Lombardy-Venetia an impressive French legacy would render difficult even a partial return to the old order but also that a preservation of Franco-Italian fixtures would go far in nourishing a partic-

ular Lombardo-Venetian regional pride. Surely Metternich was not mistaken in hoping thereby that a development of *Stammesgefühl*—a regional-national self-consciousness—might help to loosen bonds with brethren across the empire's frontiers. He, Bellegarde,[1] and others often pointed to the Italian population's preference for Franco-Italian forms which, they agreed, were better suited to Italian character than German ones. This fact alone would seem to weaken an occasionally-voiced supposition that a return to Theresian[2] methods of administration, rather than to Josephinian intentions, might have saved Austria's position in Lombardy. While both the minister and the marshal repeated the oft-told story of the successful Austrian administration in an Italy of long ago, they both at the same time admired and lamented the heritage left by the *Regno d'Italia*.[3] Thus, the emperor was eventually persuaded to follow two traditions at once by appointing—as Maria Theresia had done—a chancellor for Italian affairs in Vienna and—as Napoleon had done—a viceroy for the "royal" capital in Milan. Metternich was not alone in advocating a reconstruction of the monarchy on the principle of "unity in diversity," nor in insisting on a cultivation of regional spirit and a grant of special status to the Italian provinces. Such ideas were based on political prudence—a quality, so it seems at times, monopolized by the Staatskanzlei; yet these ideas conflicted with the organization policy—based on centralization, on conformity and equalization, and on an introduction of a German administrative system—which Kaiser Franz

---

[1] Count Heinrich Josef von Bellegarde, Austrian commander in Italy.—Ed.

[2] Referring to the more decentralized system of Maria Theresa.—Ed.

[3] The Napoleonic Kingdom of Italy.—Ed.

had already set in motion. . . . [Thus, even during the Congress of Vienna, Metternich] made a determined bid for a voice in matters of internal organization and administrative affairs and challenged the emperor's centralistic policy of conformity as politically unsound and in need of modification in order to avoid offending the feelings of the newly acquired but "national-conscious" subjects. . . .

[After the conclusion of the Second Peace of Paris in November 1815, Metternich traveled south of the Alps.] Coming to see the situation in Italy "from a point of view infinitely more liberal and congenial to the sentiments of this nation" (thus Stewart[4]), Metternich had immediately taken up the cause of meaningful Lombardo-Venetian autonomy. He strongly urged the emperor to grant effective home rule and to establish an Italian chancellery in Vienna. At the same time, he bitterly criticized the activity of the COHC[5] and demanded a thorough reappraisal of the commission's make-up and policies. Like Bellegarde, he emphasized that an elimination of prejudices between Germans and Italians, thus a better understanding between these two peoples, was a prerequisite to any improvement. The pleas of Metternich, Bellegarde and other concerned Austrians for an Italian chancellery, for a viceroy with authority, and for a Lombardo-Venetian supreme court of justice were met with imperial indecision. Only the last-named institution was approved by Kaiser Franz in 1816. In addition to a fairly autonomous Lombardo-Venetian Kingdom, Metternich proposed an Illyro-Dalmatian Kingdom—"a Southern Slavic

Reich"—for the peoples of Southern Slavic nationality and of the Roman Catholic faith. . . . In advocating the territorial integrity of Illyria-Dalmatia, the minister pointed out that the character of its people differed markedly from that of their German and Hungarian neighbors. Finally, Metternich revealed remarkable foresight by hinting that the creation of such an Illyrian kingdom, proudly ranked with the other great units of the empire, would present an effective counterweight against Russian influences and machinations among the population there. . . .

The question of [an Illyrian] "national representation" remained undecided. Metternich was known to favor it, as he had in Galicia and Lombardy-Venetia, to enable the population to develop regional pride or *Stammesstolz;* even if symbolic, a national assembly was always an expression of national personality. After all, only through a voluntary profession of such "nationality," only through a preference for being a member of the Habsburg family of "nations" could such peoples as Lombardo-Venetians, Illyrians, or Galicians loosen ties with their brethren beyond the frontier. That this meant, above all, abandoning any thought of "Germanization," Metternich emphasized often enough.

What, then, were the underlying aims of Metternich in advocating the raising of the Illyrian Provinces to such dignity? From an administrative viewpoint this plan provided neither convenience nor advantage to the central government. There was, of course, no justification for a mere revival of traditional heterogeneity and, even less, for a mere play of blocks with territories. His aims were necessarily political and concerned the structure of the entire empire: not only would the admittance of Illyria into

---

[4] Sir Charles Stewart, brother of Castlereagh and British ambassador to Austria.—Ed.

[5] For Central-Organisierungs-Hofcommission, the Austrian administrative agency for the newly acquired territories.—Ed.

the company of such territorial nations as Bohemia, Galicia, Lombardy-Venetia, and Hungary go far toward earning the gratitude and loyality of the population to the House of Habsburg, but, moreover, a political balance would be maintained among the states of the monarchy by forcing Hungary to make room for one more partner. Finally, one more step might be taken in the minister's effort to reconstitute the empire into an indissoluble bond of six or seven equal members.

Yet Metternich's plans for Illyria in 1816 implied even more. In view of his notions on the encouragement of regional nationality in Galica or Lombardy-Venetia, it would not seem unlikely that he had taken into consideration a gradual awakening of the Southern Slavs to their nationality. To have attempted, while there was still time, to guide such national feelings into forms not only acceptable but even beneficial to the monarchy would have been a policy of admirable astuteness. How better to achieve such an aim than by establishing for this nationality its own Southern Slavic realm within the empire? . . .

But Kaiser Franz did not accept this proposal and acquiesced only to a small Illyria comprised merely of the northern part of the former *Provinces Illyriennes*. There, as in the Italian provinces, respect and care for native language was practiced—albeit as an administrative necessity. Moreover, an attempt at thorough "Germanization" was more a matter of fear than fact and, despite the monarch's disinclination to grant his Italian subjects home rule, a considerable proportion of nationals served in the Lombardo-Venetian administration. With the good example of a well-governed and well-satisfied Lombardy-Venetia, Metternich had wished to bring the other Italian states to follow Austrian leadership. As it became

clear that an Italian Confederation was not to be realized, he began to seek other means to assure some coordination among Italian states. Especially as the Brindisi "disclosures" rekindled old fears of a nation-wide conspiracy to achieve national union under a constitutional regime, the need for some all-Italian controls was made obvious. Although soon played down, the "plot" helped in establishing the Central Observation Agency, a bureau designed to spot trouble throughout Italy and which, so Metternich hoped, would help safeguard the Italian repose that Austria needed in order to fulfill its program and promises. Because obviously the emperor's visit to Italy and Illyria had resulted not in those positive measures Metternich had hoped for but rather in increased discontent, the minister felt called upon to seek a new approach to a general solution. . . .

In 1817 Metternich resumed efforts to settle the Lombardo-Venetian problem satisfactorily and permanently, once again pressing the emperor to comply with "national wishes" for home rule and to appoint at least a viceroy and an Italian chancellor. Simultaneously, he stressed that Austria could maintain its position as a major power and as a bulwark against disorder only if "morally strong in our interior." He considered these two points as joint issues. The need for removing temporary authority—i.e., the COHC—in the reacquired lands and aligning them with the other areas of the empire under one central authority gave impetus to and was combined with an even more ambitious program: the reorganization of the empire's central administration down to the regional level in a manner best suited to strengthen the monarchy against the perils of the future. Here, the idea of centralization was ruled out except where demanded by a common purpose of the various member states. Moreover, according to Metternich, the empire's full strength was to be developed by an inner political balance resulting from equal treatment (not equalization) of all "nations" of the Austrian *Völker-familie*. A reorganization was all the more necessary because this was not the case, Hungary having too much, other areas too little to say. The idea *unity in diversity* and the equality of all regions was to be demonstrated by equally ranked chancelleries, designed to represent each area's special regional-national interests. They were to be subordinated to a ministry of the interior acting in the interest of the empire as a whole. According to Prince Dietrichstein[6] (whose own proposals spelled out Austria's needs much more openly), Metternich originally proposed six chancelleries: for Bohemia-Galicia, Inner-Austria, Illyria, Lombardy-Venetia, Hungary, and Transylvania. But then Metternich decided to defer action on the two last named chancelleries to avoid jeopardizing what he emphatically labelled his "first step."

Kaiser Franz agreed to his foreign minister's limited program at most half-heartedly, and proceeded to despoil it of its underlying ideas by arbitrarily combining the Austrian and Illyrian chancelleries; he did not even bother to name a chancellor for this combination, and left the number of appointed chancellors actually at two—the centralist-minded Lazansky[7] and the reluctant Mellerio.[8] Moreover, the emperor refused to accept the fact that his *Hofkanzlei* had become a *ministry of the interior*. Only Lombardy-Venetia appeared to receive tangible benefit from the new system through the appointment of a viceroy and a chancellor. There especially, Metternich meant to make the most of the meager results in the hope of convincing the sensitive public as well as the distrustful emperor that all sides would benefit from the new measures. But neither the reports of a momentary enthusiasm in Lombardy-Venetia nor the fear of disappointing an expectant public moved the emperor to magnanimity. Despite frequent pleas from Metternich and Bubna to implement the December 24 patent, he refused to grant Viceroy Ranier[9] or Chancellor Mellerio the authority their positions called for. That Austria had nothing more to offer its Italian subjects other than this imperfect permanent solution was considered a breach of faith; apathy, disillusion, a marked deterioration in public mood followed, and Austrian rule in Italy continued, more than ever lacking the consent of the governed. . . .

Metternich must be credited with having the ideas and striving to open the emperor's eyes to an admirably sensible program—a program almost fascinating in the way it anticipated much of what was arrived at in futile hindsight decades—even a century—later. That this first official attempt to deal with the idea of nationality in the Austrian Empire failed does not deprive it of its own historic significance; it is really beside the point whether the conjecture—what might have been had Metternich's reorganization program been realized—leaves one with feelings of skepticism or of sadness at lost opportunities. However, although Metternich had the program, he could

---

[6] Prince Franz Josef von Dietrichstein, retired Austrian official who maintained a keen interest in public affairs.—Ed.

[7] Count Prokop Lazansky, president of the COHC.—Ed.

[8] Count Mellerio, designated to head the Italian chancellery in Vienna.—Ed.

[9] Archduke Rainer, younger brother of Emperor Francis.—Ed.

not sell it to his monarch. The question arises whether Metternich, had he mobilized all the force of his personality and authority, could have pushed his measures through despite imperial obduracy. To be sure, the emperor had admitted his limitations and yielded to Metternich in external affairs as bitter experience had taught him to do; it was otherwise with internal matters, where he discerned no urgency, much less crisis. At least with home affairs he intended to act the absolute and paternal monarch and to achieve an ideal inherited from his uncle Joseph: to conduct personally all affairs in his domain through a centralized administration. But with repeated, and mostly unsuccessful, approaches Metternich had reached the limit of the emperor's as well as of his own patience and the minister was not one to run full tilt against a wall. With all his charm, he would have been the first to agree that selfdenial—that is, risking his position for his convictions— was rather pointless if it meant depriving Austria of its one capable statesman, one to whom it owed so much. Anyway, Kaiser Franz was not to be argued with or threatened with resignation as Wilhelm I was to be by Bismarck; he would have accepted it, most likely, with regret but without hesitation. The decisive point is that in these years Metternich was not all-powerful and that his lack of authority in internal policy fairly absolves him from its errors. . . .

VIKTOR BIBL (1870–1947) was for almost two decades between the world wars a colleague of Srbik at the University of Vienna and, like him, an ardent Pan-Germanist. About Metternich, however, they completely disagreed, Bibl holding him to be a wholly destructive force—a "demon," to use his term—for Austria, Germany, and Europe. In several major works on Metternich Bibl singled out Srbik's views for special condemnation, as is evident in this selection, which argues that Metternich deliberately set Austria on a disastrous course merely to maintain himself in office. Bibl's style is polemical but his knowledge of Metternich is based on extensive research.*

Viktor Bibl

The Destructive Demon of Austria

The gravest of all the reproaches that can be raised against the Chancellor, however, is the suspicion that in reality he was not at all "blind to the forces around him" and "devoid of ideas," that rather, against his own better judgment, he pursued a policy disastrous for Austria. Is one to believe that a gifted man like him did not really perceive what even simpler heads at the Viennese court, such as Archduke John, had long since seen: that it was a vain effort to oppose the world-shaking power of the new ideas? He himself admitted in 1820, "The times move forward amid storms: to try to tame their violence would be futile endeavor." And in the same year he said, "My life has fallen in a dreadful period. I have come into the world either too early or too late; now I feel myself good for absolutely nothing. Earlier, I would have enjoyed the times; later, I might have served in building up anew; today, I spend my life propping up the rotted structures."

But why did Metternich regard it as his task to prop up the rotted structures instead of following the great example of his Rhenish compatriot Stein and rebuilding? He had perfectly good ideas—as when he advised the tsar in 1816 that powerful armies were too heavy a burden on the national economy and a danger to the peace of Europe. Naturally, he said it so that the rival in the Orient would leave Austria alone; he himself, however, to the despair of Kolowrat, the minister

*From Viktor Bibl, *Metternich, der Dämon Österreichs* (Leipzig and Vienna: Johannes Günther Verlag, 1936), pp. 358-362, omitting the original footnotes. Translated by Keith Mostofi and Enno E. Kraehe.

in charge of financial affairs, maintained an almost continuous mobilization and made a shambles of the internal resources of the monarchy. And how splendid too was the advice he gave his emperor the following year, that he should eliminate the causes of unrest in the kingdom of Lombardy-Venetia, stop the police persecutions, and try to win the public opinion of Italy for the imperial state! Yet a few years later we see him directing the proceedings against the Italian patriots with a positive zeal. So at that time—1817 —he had for once dropped the terribly one-sided point of view that every movement originated with "secret societies" —the "original lie," as Gentz put it— but evidently he did not prevail with Emperor Francis.

And what kind of apparatus was necessary to carry on this struggle against the *Zeitgeist?* It was really no exaggeration when Hormayr[1] remarked, "Insane amounts were squandered on it." But with what result? The finance ministry, which had tried for years and decades to put a stop to the extravagance indulged in by the state chancellery in behalf of the secret service, correctly noted a few days after the March catastrophe[2] that this ever so expensive secret police always failed at the decisive moment. It was taken by surprise just as much by the Italian revolution of 1821 as by the Galician one of 1846 and the March Revolution. Only a few years after the Congress of Vienna Wilhelm von Humboldt, under the influence of the Carlsbad Decrees, had declared, "All mere police activity gradually fails in its purpose; it makes the evil worse at the root and never succeeds in stopping all outbreaks or even discovering them."

---

[1] Baron Josef von Hormayr, Austrian official.—Ed.
[2] That is, the outbreak of revolution in Vienna in March 1848.—Ed.

At that time this was already the general opinion, so to speak, but Metternich clung to his system even when Emperor Francis, who could not have imagined an Austria without it, was no longer alive.

In his memoirs, Franz Grillparzer gives his view of Metternich's inflexibility after Francis' death, explaining that the former grumbler about the emperor's narrow-minded policy, now that he was old himself, continued in the "old rut" out of laziness and "dignified the measures adopted against his will with the honorary title of a system." In practice, though, the pliant chancellor had already made this system his own during the emperor's lifetime, precisely because his complaints had been to no avail. To the Russian chancellor Nesselrode, who had made the excuse that he had been unable to put his point of view across, he exclaimed, "Either you are minister or you are not!" —but he did not act that way himself. He avoided any struggle with his imperial master that would have cost him his post.

Did the sum total of Metternich's ideas for the preservation of the state thus really narrow down solely to the idea of maintaining himself in his post? His physician Dr. Jäger testified that never in his life had he come into contact with a more complete egoist than the State Chancellor. Thus it would seem comprehensible that Metternich put his own welfare ahead of that of the imperial state and for purely personal reasons pursued a policy which, according to his own conviction, must lead to Austria's downfall. That people believed him capable of such frivolity is shown by the words put into his mouth from all sides: *"Après nous le déluge!"* A remark of his closest colleague, Gentz, also made the rounds: "It'll last out Metternich and me."

To this was added the accusation

openly raised against him that he took money from everywhere and, above all, was regularly in the pay of Russia. It was known that Gentz accepted payments— and he made no secret of it himself. That was what brought Grillparzer to remark, "When a superior tolerates gift-taking by his subordinates, he is usually not very particular about such matters himself, and the enormous expenditures of the prince, his purchase of estates—he, who took over his father's estate in a state of bankruptcy—clearly suggests diplomatic *pour boire . . ."*

Whether the terrible suspicion that Metternich betrayed the interests of his state for his own interests was well-founded or not—about that one can argue; it is enough that people universally believed it, that they believed him capable of everything, even the worst. And one thing is certain: the *grand seigneur,* evidently following the principle attributed to Louis XV's predecessor, "I am the State!" supported a portion of his fancy tastes from the funds of the already seriously impoverished state. He furnished the state chancellery, where he had his living quarters, with "extravagant magnificence," used the most costly French silks as tapestries for it, and, unconcerned about the protests of the monarch and the finance ministry, calmly went on building until in the end the large sum of 88,000 gulden was provided him by Francis "as a favor." He had the painters Lieder and Thomas Ender ride as cabinet-couriers, the one to Paris, the other to Ischl, and in this way could the more cheaply acquire the reputation of being a patron of the arts. And not least, in his frequent financial difficulties he knew how to help himself to short-term state loans. Whether that always occurred with the tacit approval of the monarch— who can prove that today! Again, enough

that people spoke rather openly of the "unorthodox" procedure, and the "misappropriation" that was carried on with the funds allocated from the state chancellery was openly protested. One could excuse this with Metternich's "inability to judge the value of money," but in an "ordered state" such disorder was quite out of place. And all that in an era when even the court took some account of the democratic tendency of the times. As Kübeck[3] complained, the Prince was considered as "representative of all the abuses and presumptions of *haute société,"* and that was certainly not conducive to making him more beloved of the people, who in the 'forties had to face severe economic hardship.

The hatred, however, which raged against Metternich in all circles, high and low, constituted a heavy burden for state and dynasty. That the Prince defied this fact, which could not have been unknown to him, and even on March 13 put off his stormily demanded resignation until blood had flowed and a street brawl had become a real revolution, was fateful for Austria. Thus, on him falls the full blame for the outbreak of the March Revolution with all its catastrophic consequences, the increasing difficulties with which Francis Joseph had to contend and which, in spite of the most strenuous and unremitting labor, he was unable to master. The peaceful, steady development of the imperial state which a revitalization of the estates structure at the right time would seem to have guaranteed was prevented by Metternich and with it a freer movement of peoples in the framework of the Danubian monarchy. The absolutist unitary state, a consequence of the preceding

---

[3] Baron Karl Friedrich von Kübeck, Austrian councillor and finance expert, confidant of Metternich.—Ed.

revolution, brought forth the "conflict of peoples" which crippled the internal strength of the Habsburg empire. Metternich's unfortunate German and Italian policies led to the fateful days of Solferino[4] and Königgrätz,[5] to the long delayed opening of the Eastern Question —which he did not want to see touched— and to the world war.

Metternich was not the "conservative" principle; everywhere, he had a disintegrating effect on the authority of the state, sowed distrust and dissension between prince and people, prince and ministers, and finally in Austria itself he put the axe to the edifice of the state—with full justification his own associates in 1830 characterized him as a "revolutionary." Neither was he the guardian of the European peace; everywhere he sowed discord, and the armed peace that reigned after the Congress of Vienna hindered the work of construction no less than a number of wars. Above all, however, the artificially repressed forces and problems burst in on Europe with devastating violence. The expanse of ruins which the collapse of November 1918 left behind is in the final analysis the work of Prince Metternich.

He was truly the—demon of Austria.

---

[4] Site of Austrian defeat by France and Sardinia-Piedmont, 1859.—Ed.

[5] Site of Austrian defeat by Prussia, 1866.—Ed.

Ever since the publication in 1950 of his two large volumes on the nationality problem, ROBERT A. KANN (b. 1906) has been a leading authority on Austrian history. Originally trained in Vienna as a lawyer, Kann migrated to the United States in 1938 to resume university studies, this time at Columbia and in history. He is a professor at Rutgers University and a past chairman of the Conference Group for Central European History. This selection from a book published in 1960 offers profound insights into the problems of Metternich's Austria. True, Kann says, Metternich knew that inaction would ultimately lead to disaster—as Bibl charges—but the alternatives would have been repugnant to his values and might have made things worse. This is tragedy, not cynicism.*

Robert A. Kann

Statesman in Tragic Impasse

The State Chancellor was faced with the difficult task of settling the gradually evolving problem of political nationalism without impairing the key position of an Austrian empire in the center of a European combination of powers. Whether rightly or wrongly, but certainly not without reasons worthy of careful consideration, he believed that the German element in the monarchy would be the most likely to hold together the heterogeneous realms of the Habsburg power. Living as he did in a time that was not yet familiar with the devices and implications of various systems of national autonomy and the character of ethnic nationalism, he knew at least that neither a system of streamlined Josephine centralism nor one of federalism on the basis of the historic-political entities crossing national boundaries could offer a fully satisfactory solution. He realized further that the Hungarian question represented problems per se which could not be treated on the same basis as those of lesser entities. He has been frequently, and on the whole rightly, criticized for his profound disregard of the Italian national issue and at points, with less justification, for his uninspiring attitude toward the complex problem of the German Confederation. In fairness to Metternich it should be pointed out that the Austro-Italian provinces, Galicia, and the Germanies could

*From Robert A. Kann, *A Study in Austrian Intellectual History from Late Baroque to Romanticism* (New York: Frederick A. Praeger, 1960), pp. 289–294, omitting the original footnotes. Reprinted by permission of Thames and Hudson, Ltd., and Frederick A. Praeger, Inc.

not be seen by him primarily from the angle of the national issue but as outposts and bastions of the precarious Austrian Great Power position hemmed in by Russia, Prussia, and France. Neither should the positive element of an in many ways passive and unimaginative nationality policy be overlooked: a timid and suspicious attitude in regard to the national problem in general prevented at least an equally dangerous deviation in the opposite direction—that is, subservience to any specific national force, to the detriment of the others. In the light of the sinister Pan-Slav ideologies then emerging in Russia and the possible dangers of a Pan-German course, which in Metternich's time would have been emotionally much stronger than in Joseph's, this point must not be overlooked.

Early vacillations notwithstanding, Metternich also avoided the error of assuming the existence of an Austrian nation to be promoted almost inevitably by way of an artificial over-all Austrian national idea in a Jacobin or ethnic sense. In the foreground of the Chancellor's political thinking appeared now the concept of the Austrian state and the Austrian-state idea embracing many nationalities, bound together by a German-directed cultural and administrative superstructure under the supreme union of the crown. This may still have appeared as a controversial concept to many, but nobody could claim that it was an arbitrary one. It certainly was not a constructive approach to the national problem; on the other hand, this concept did not eliminate the historical realities of the traditions of the Habsburg lands. It denied the notion of the integrated, fully centralized state, but in Srbik's words, "we can call the Austria which Metternich looked for the decentralized unified state." Metternich finally denied in the political sphere the whole evolutionary idea of constitutional government in the modern sense. This held true not only on the central level but on the lower one of the historical political entities as well—partial concessions in the administrative field notwithstanding. As Srbik again rightly points out, the Hungarian exceptions and the concessions to Magyarism imply here only recognition of an existing force, a force based on traditional constitutional government, but not on popular sovereignty. It may be added that it means only a concession to a force too strong to overcome; it does not mean insight into the necessity of reform but insight into the limitations of executive central power.

This lack of spiritual readiness for genuine reform applies of course not only to the Hungarian question. Only feeble attempts were made to create an imperial consultative council in legislative affairs in conjunction with a ministerial conference to deal with administrative agenda. Metternich's provisions for separate advisory consultants in Hungarian affairs and a division of a Ministry of Interior into Bohemian-Moravian-Galician, Austrian (i.e., German-Austrian), Illyrian (Southern Slav and Italian) chancelleries quite apart from the autonomous Hungarian administration did not succeed either. They were weakened in their organization by imperial ordinance, and even more so by imperial practice. Yet even if the projects of the State Chancellor had been fully realized, they would by no means have resulted in national autonomous and constitutional government in the modern sense. Again from the standpoint of immanent criticism, Metternich cannot be blamed for the rejection of principles that collided with the basic philosophy of his system. It was naïve to assume, however, that a feeble and soulless approximation to a separation-of-power system and federal-representative organization could bridge the abyss between the principles of the system and the rising demands of modern ideas. It is not in the formulation and execution of the policy of nis system, which will always be respected in its way as a model of clear thinking, but in his pseudo-concessions and attempts to compromise superficially with new conditions that the Chancellor was at his worst.

This applies also to the unsuccessful attempts to revise rather than to reform the Hungarian Estates constitution, the failure to co-operate in time with the enlightened and moderate leaders of the nation, Count Stephen Széchenyi and Francis Deák. Though perhaps in a less conspicuous way, the same is true of the series of lost opportunities to support the Bohemian and German-Austrian moderate enlightened reformers Count Leo Thun, Francis Palacký, Victor von Andrian-Werburg, and others of equally distinguished rank. In Metternich's time, far-reaching, though to be sure imperfect solutions based on a modified concept of the historical-political entities might still have been feasible. Necessary evolutionary revisions of these solutions later on might still have been technically difficult but, since the factor of national pressure would have been greatly relieved, by no means impossible. Neither feasible nor possible, however, was the notion of tolerating up to a point the evolution of cultural-humanitarian nationalism among the empire's Slavonic peoples as a counterweight against Magyarism and Eastern Pan-Slavism, and of expecting that such movements could be stopped short of the evolution of political rights. Here the system profoundly lacked insight into the factor of continuity in history which, in several aspects of foreign policy, was one of its assets. Piecemeal reforms like the

Hungarian-language regulations of 1846, which still had to resort to the Latin expedient, and the temporary and in a revolutionary way backfiring support of Ruthenian national rights against Polish nationalism do not change this picture substantially. Thus altogether, many of the Chancellor's and his advisers' subtle reflections notwithstanding, the practical results of the system's sophisticated national policy flowed into the same channel as the emperor's simple and stubborn rejection of the whole issue.

Two main arguments can be brought forward here, however, in defense of the system's policy. For one thing, the results of the experiments of the two following generations in the field of Austrian nationalism cannot claim better results than Metternich's negative policy. If measured by the tragic final outcome, they are in a way far worse. In the light of the principle of continuity in history, this line of reasoning is deceptive. The problem of nationalism in Metternich's time in the monarchy was not yet the deadly issue that it was to become for later generations. There was probably no real chance of settling it even then. But there was a better chance of easing it and keeping it under control before it had assumed its integral character and had become more ominously linked with increased external imperialist pressure from abroad. The system cannot be condemned for having failed to find nonexistent perfect solutions. It can be blamed, however, for having underrated the dangerous potentialities of the national problem.

The second point to be considered in defense of Metternich on this particular issue carries much greater weight. The national question, as a genuine or alleged expression of the will of the people, is inextricably linked with the problem of popular sovereignty. Many a champion of the national idea had acted quite sincerely in the service of this issue; some others, particularly in the period of integral nationalism, have exploited it for dictatorial purposes. Yet everyone has paid at least lip-service to it. That Metternich was above such hypocrisy is certainly to his credit. Here the observations made by Heinrich Heine in 1852, though intended in a more general sense, are pertinent:

Indeed, we might fight against Austria and fight heroically until death, sword in hand; yet most deeply we feel that we are not justified in abusing this power in words. Austria was always a frank, honest enemy, who has never denied her fight against Liberalism and who has never stopped it intermittently. Metternich has never flirted with the goddess of freedom; never in the fear of his heart has he played the demagogue. He has never sung Arndt's songs to Berlin beer; he has never practiced gymnastics on the Hasenheide; he has never affected sanctimonious piety. He has never shed tears with the political prisoners while he held them in chains. One always knew where one stood with him; one knew that one had to watch out for him, and one did. He was always a reliable man who neither deceived us by gracious looks nor infuriated us by private malice. One knew that he did not act out of either love or petty hatred, but grandly in the spirit of his system, to which Austria has remained faithful for three centuries. This is the system for which Austria has fought against the Reformation; this is the system for which Austria has opened the fight against the revolution. . . .

This is no negligible testimony to the character of Metternich the man on the part of one whose political philosophy was diametrically opposed to that of the Chancellor. In a way it is even more than that. It is by implication a testimony to the work of Metternich the statesman as well. As a statesman he could not be expected to act against his principles, even though it would have shown foresight on his part if he had made serious compromises not only in the case of the national issue but in other issues as well. He could have gone along with national reforms on the basis of the historical-political entities without seriously endangering the *raison d'être* of his system. But nobody would have been able to guarantee him that reform could be stopped at this point. Even in Metternich's time such a contingency seemed questionable. Further evolution in the direction of ethnic nationalism linked to the organization of popular representation within the frame of democratic constitutional government might have prevented revolution, but, according to Metternich's philosophy, only at the price of heavy ideological sacrifice. Moreover, the whole subtle system of foreign relations so brilliantly executed in regard to France, so precariously maintained in view of the development of the problems of the German Confederation, Greece, Naples, Russo-Polish aspirations, and other conflict zones, might well have been upset. Could Metternich really have been expected to be willing to take such a course, which might have diminished the dangers of an as yet uncertain revolution but which would inevitably have entailed changes that to Metternich were hardly less objectionable and dangerous than revolution itself? The answer to this question is a clear "no," a "no" that exonerates Metternich the man, justifies him even as statesman from the standpoint of immanent criticism, but in this instance condemns the system, which by implication considers both evolutionary democratic reform and revolution as equally objectionable alternatives, possibly even as equally great dangers. Metternich rightly rejected and feared revolution and its possible consequences, but he would have considered the reformed Austria that might have prevented revolution with a certain degree of probability not worth fighting for and well worth fighting against. This is the true, inevitable, and tragic impasse into which Metternich's leadership had steered Austria in regard to the most important issues facing the body politic.

VEIT VALENTIN (1885–1947) was one of many scholars who left Germany in the wake of the Nazi revolution and enriched learning in other lands. An outspoken liberal democrat, he lost his posts at the Berlin School of Economics and the German archives at Potsdam, taught for a time at the University of London, and finally came to the United States. His principal contribution to scholarship consists of two stout volumes dealing in great breadth and detail with the German revolutions of 1848. Although the English edition of this work is severely abridged, this selection from it is uncut and true to the original eloquent indictment of Metternich by a man who shared the liberal values of 1848.*

Veit Valentin

Metternich Guilty

It was neither Franz nor Ferdinand who determined Austria's destiny. The fate of Austria, of Germany, of all Europe was summed up for many a year in the one name—Metternich. The revolutionary movement of 1848–49 can only be understood in the light of this man's work and personality. It was directed against the very nature of the man, against his spirit, his principles, his "system." He who defends Metternich, condemns the Revolution. To defend the Revolution is to damn him. Both need to be *understood*.

Two generations of German, Italian, Slavonic youth hated under the name of Metternich everything which seemed to them deserving of hatred. The curses of Grillparzer and Lenau[1] were levelled

against his system. Until our own day he was in the company of the damned. The new European feeling of the post-war period sought to reinstate him. What is the truth about Metternich?

"The Rhine flows in my veins," wrote the old prince, as he looked down from the heights of his home on the Johannis hill for the last time, shortly before his death. Even in Vienna, despite all the grave dignity that encompassed a State chancellor, he had remained a Rhinelander of the old country: charming, easygoing, tasteful, fond of conversation—in politics, a cosmopolitan European. His comrades at the University had had a nickname for him—"Fin, faux, fanfaron"[2] —he was agreeable, complacent to a fault,

---

[1] Nikolaus Lenau, Austrian poet.—Ed.

[2] Roughly: "sly, deceptive braggart."—Ed.

---

*From Veit Valentin, *1848: Chapters in German History* (New York: Archon Books, 1965), pp. 14–19. Reprinted by permission of George Allen and Unwin, Ltd., and Archon Books, Inc.

a man of talents, but even more vain than gifted. The French Revolution of 1789 had robbed the princely house of Metternich, like many another, of home and property: was it not inevitable that he should hate this revolution? Must he not love a conservative stability, such as he found in England? In self-determination of peoples, freedom of nations, democracy, he saw only the destruction of what had been and a hindrance to quiet development: there was only one answer to revolutionary demands and all their militant unrest, and his professors had already taught young Metternich that answer: *Pax Christiana,* European Republic.

Metternich conquered Napoleon. Determined, polished, and without prejudice, quietly crafty, he studied the man of destiny of his epoch. He did not suffer, nor rise up against him with heroic imprudence, full of wrath against the Emperor, as Freiherr vom Stein had done. Early in life, Metternich was already a master of preparing the next step, he was neither particularly courageous nor especially energetic. He liked to talk in riddles and to employ roundabout methods; he revered the power of money and high position, and above all he had confidence in himself. He temporized, employed finesse of every kind, played against Napoleon, with him and round about him for a long time—too long, for at last no one knew who was the cheat and who the cheated.

But he conquered the heroic man of blood; he, the fine gentleman, squire of dames, frivolous, playful tactician, a man who was hated by all serious moralists and upright men to whom their politics were a matter of faith. But it was he who achieved his end and not they: a powerful Austrian Imperial State, soaring high over the heads of Germany, Italy, and the Slavs, heart of an anti-revolutionary Central Europe, allied with Russia and with England, determined to hold off France and keep Prussia small and feeble. Undisturbed, Metternich allowed France to swallow Alsace and Lorraine, indifferently he renounced the Rhenish influence accruing from of old to the House of Hapsburg: he thought concentration more important. The Imperial State was a little Europe in itself and the German Federation and the Holy Alliance made this little Europe an axis of the greater Europe beyond its borders. The imperial name continued to carry on the universalism of the old in a new form. The old empire had been "holy" and "Roman"; the new system of the Imperial State of Austria was holy and Roman in a peculiar new manner of its own; it was the very embodiment of counter-revolution.

Metternich took pleasure in observing spiders and admired the cruel cleverness of their cross-threads. He wove his own nets over all that made up his world. He was the first Court- and State-Chancellor since Prince Kaunitz: noble and nonchalant, finest flower of his time and his class, an eternal fixed smile upon his lips. When he laughed, which was seldom, people were horrified at the Mephistophelian leer that turned his features to a grimace. His mild blue eye seldom darted a sudden lightning out of that polite mask; his nasal voice had no resonance; as he grew old he was always lecturing in long perorations. In extreme old age he had almost acquired the "Hapsburg lip."

Metternich achieved all that could be achieved by *esprit* and *raison,* in which the eighteenth century always excelled the nineteenth. He was always busy, business was to him a living thing. How easily he apprehended everything, not only its material content, but the very thoughts of those who reported to him! He at once, all too quickly, visualized the whole situation in agreeable fashion; he was fond of improvizing and did it well, and so, in spite of his many activities, he always had plenty of time, time for people and for good stories, for travel, books, enjoyment of every kind, for rarities, even for the serious study of natural sciences; he loved to lard his talk with scientific idiom. He was most successful and this seemed to him to prove that he was always right; thus the master diplomatist fancied himself also a master strategist and historian; the naïveté of this over-estimation of his powers marks the boundaries of his personality. Sensual and sly, he took what he could get, but poured forth edifying talk about his warmth of heart. In essence he was a genius of cool reason, a cold and mightly prosaist of conservatism, an arrogant man of possessions who protected and revered all men of property, an enlightened great lord, whose soul revolted against everything warm and young, everything mysterious and mystical, everything spectacularly heroic, all simple faith, the oppressed and the fanatical.

Metternich was no "Social Conservative" as were Disraeli and Bismarck in a later age, but a reactionary, although the most brilliant and elegant of all reactionaries of his day. He led the great counterblast against the revolutionary movement. But the Revolution hit back and swept him away. He may have patronized technical progress, economic development, and the spread of communications—but he did it as a descendant of the old police state. Everything new in Austria was suppressed wherever possible—although the new was too many-coloured and powerful to be capable of suppression.

Metternich's foreign policy preserved the peace, they say. But it reached its height before the July revolution. When one congress followed on the heels of the last, in the 'twenties, Europe was politically active, legitimist, united against every national and liberal tendency. The turning-point was Greece's fight for freedom. England turned her back on the "system." Then Metternich, acting upon a correct instinct, proposed to make war upon the France of the July revolution. Archduke Karl proved that a war would be impossible for Austria, with her financial deficit and her neglected army. It was at this point that Metternich's system might really be considered as shattered to the core. The period until the outbreak of the Revolution of 1848 was the merciful interregnum of an aristocratic façade hiding an actual state of bankruptcy. It was a period rich in humiliations and defeats, alternating with momentary successes. A keen observer such as Count Arnim, the Prussian minister, could not fail to observe the deep internal weakness of Metternich and his system. He wrote thus, six months before the outbreak of the Revolution of 1848:

The man in whom the power of Austria is centralized, has one foot in the grave. His old intellectual strength is broken, and although as a diplomatist he is still apparently at his height, he is no longer statesman enough, nor has he the State sufficiently firm in hand to master the present state of things. He has had to endure many a mortification of late, plans have gone astray, old opponents, among them Count Kolowrat, have been singled out by the Emperor and honoured by visits and so on—all this has embittered the last days of his glorious career and broken him up more quickly than would otherwise have been the case.

Metternich attempted to comfort himself and others for the mighty innovations which were sweeping Europe, including Austria, by setting up a number of precepts, threadbare though they were. Apparently as calm and dignified as ever, still impressive as a highly-cultivated man of the world, he hoped to be able to maintain his position by means of his studied carelessness, his supple cleverness, a tactician turning weakness to a weapon. His contemporaries undoubtedly suspected the pettiness of the mighty man, although he understood so admirably how to mask it behind great principles.

Metternich's Austrian Imperial State was a little Europe which aspired to be the heart of Greater Europe—a small Europe led by Germany under the visible sign of German claims to hegemony. Metternich could preserve his European position only as long as he could succeed in keeping all Germany at his back. If Germany were to set herself up against the Imperial State of Austria, the crisis would have come. In July 1847, the Chancellor expounded his view of things very characteristically to Count Arnim, the Prussian minister. "The French cabinet has called Austria an Italian power and deduces from this an eventual right to intervene. Austria has Italian provinces, to be sure, but she is not an Italian power." There were only three nationalities, said the Prince, the Germanic, the Latin, and the Slavonic. "Austria is a realm which embraces peoples of various nationalities under its sovereignty, but as realm she has only one nationality. This is the German—she is German as a matter of history, as the point of junction of all her provinces and by virtue of her civilization."

If all the vital powers in the Imperial State must turn against the patriarchal central guardianship, then they were at the same time warring against the German element which it represented. And if the German element desired freedom, it must shatter the basis of the Imperial State. In this tangle of contradictions we have at once the bitterest denunciation and the only justification of Metternich and his system.

At the end of World War II, when the authorities in occupied Austria needed a replacement for the one-time Nazi apologist Heinrich von Srbik as professor of modern history at the University of Vienna, they turned to a man the Nazis had earlier sent to a concentration camp: HUGO HANTSCH. A Catholic priest and author of numerous works on the Habsburg monarchy, Hantsch (b. 1895) is best known for a two-volume history of Austria which emphasizes not its German character but its supranational tradition rooted in Christianity. The excerpt which follows is taken from this work. Metternich is not the main subject, but the author's European viewpoint and his ironic treatment of the revolutionary hopes and programs leave no doubt that he exonerates the ousted statesman. Thus, despite their common hostility to Nazism, Hantsch and Valentin arrive at opposite assessments of Metternich.*

Hugo Hantsch

Metternich Not Guilty

"The Springtime of Peoples"—that was the phrase they coined for those days of struggle for a new way of life. Actually, it is difficult to form an adequate idea of the joy, the enthusiasm, and the overpowering optimism that seized the men of that day. In the memories of many contemporaries, these fateful days of March 1848 seemed like one great celebration of brotherhood and goodwill, filled with impetuous hopes for the blessings of a new era. Often there was a veritable ecstasy of joy which touched almost everyone, like a storm roaring in from an unknown quarter and roaring off again no one knows where. Along with the feeling of having been delivered from an oppressive nightmare went the blissful awareness of being in possession of oneself, a bursting forth of pent-up energy, a beckoning intimation of spring which stole over every heart and seemed to unite it with every other heart and especially affected the young. It was as though mankind had been transformed by a magic wand, transported by a magic word into another world where, overwhelmed by the wealth of inrushing experiences and full of joyful anticipation, it sought inquisitively to orient itself. The magic word was "constitution."

It was not as if everyone who had the

*From Hugo Hantsch, *Die Geschichte Österreichs,* 4th ed. (2 vols.; Graz, Vienna, and Cologne: Verlag Styria, 1968), vol. 2, pp. 321–325. Translated by Keith Mostofi and Enno E. Kraehe.

word on his lips knew what it meant. Marvelous and unrealizable expectations were bound up in it. Most people expected from it release from their personal problems; yet all of them were right in thinking that a new era had dawned, that the stream of history had carried them to a verdant bank, and that they must seize with both hands the new land that had sprung up so luxuriantly before their intoxicated eyes. Constitution was freedom, a coveted and simply unattainable commodity, but it signified fulfillment, joyous, unhampered striving, and hence blissful existence. People had a fantastic notion of "liberty": only a few were aware that liberty also meant responsibility, that there must be a law to define its limits or it would no longer be a blessing but a calamity. To set these limits through their own strength and sense of duty; not to be bullied by the external forces that had burst their bonds but instead, through religion, community spirit and high-mindedness in the adjustment and subordination of individual differences, to curb the lurking hydra of egoism and the tryanny of class and individual selfishness—that was the great task of the constitution, of self-imposed law, and its duly authorized elected guardians.

"Constitution"—that meant the recognition of the people as participants in the power structure, the unassailable position of the people collectively as the highest organ of independent will and purpose; certainly it brought a feeling of pride, a majestic dignity, but it was also an ideal that human weakness could all too easily distort and disfigure. Constitution and freedom—those were great words. The era venerated and became intoxicated with the word that hitherto had been denied to it and which now gushed forth like a raging stream in passionate oratory or in the unmistakable style of slick journalism. Overnight the word became a power, an instrument in the hands of more or less conscientious men. It turned its back on the past and proclaimed a happy future.

Like an eagle ready to strike, the word circled over Chancellor Clemens Metternich, his "system," and his principles. It condemned not only the man himself but through him a whole era, a social order, and an entire political structure. It took no notice of his positive achievements for the peace of Europe and of Austria, of the undeniable services he had performed in the struggle against Napoleon for the restoration of Europe, in the struggle against the spirit of the French Revolution incarnate in the conqueror, who had made himself heard with the thunder of cannon, had commanded obedience at the point of blood-spattered bayonets, and had transformed the lofty human ideal of liberty, equality, and fraternity into a weapon of destruction and enslavement. People completely overlooked the fact that by no means every charge that could justifiably be brought against the pre-March system of government belonged in the long indictment which the year 1848 and liberalism presented to the Chancellor; in many respects, he himself was the prisoner of a governmental system, or rather a governmental machine, which Joseph II had set in motion. People might garland the statue of the emperor who had created the all-powerful state and endowed it with an arrogant and inflexible bureaucratic instrument, but they damned the statesman who had preserved this state and, in doing so, availed himself of this instrument. People did not know how many well-intentioned proposals for changes and reforms emanating from the upper levels of the bureaucracy and even from the office of the State Chancellor had rebounded without effect off the mean, timid, and autocratic character of Francis I, and they scarcely mentioned the most serious mistake Metternich had made: by rigidly adhering to untenable principles, he had placed the state in the hands of a regent who could not govern and yet did not have the energy to compensate for this weakness by a broader and more open system of participation in government, but instead left matters in a dangerous state of suspense. An absolute state with an incompetent ruler at its head is a contradiction and a danger, for invariably in such cases a power struggle will flare up, a paralysis of authority will set in, and the confidence of subjects will be badly shaken. Such are among the psychological preconditions of every revolution.

Nevertheless, even under other circumstances the revolution would not have come to a halt at Austria's borders; it concerned matters of principle, and broke out first in the very South-German states which had the most liberal constitutions, that is, where a political consciousness was most highly developed.

The revolutionary movement in Europe took different courses according to the particular level of development of states and peoples, their character and temperament. Its immediate goals varied. A revolution that arose from an atmosphere prepared well in advance, as was the case in France, must look entirely different from one, as in Austria, without a clear and well-defined program, without organization, arising more from emotion, as it were—although it might be observed in this connection that no genuine revolution is based on a detailed program. In Vienna there was a spontaneous uprising that had no real leadership and succeeded only because a weak, shortsighted, overconfident, and unprepared government

retired from the field and, misled by the signal fires shooting up all around, called it quits before the confusion of the first day was overcome. Overnight the people found themselves in possession of a degree of power which the day before they had not even aspired to, but once aware of their power, they were determined to maintain and extend it. The unexpected successes of the first tumultuous day determined that the old state structure would collapse from decay. But where was the master builder capable of erecting a new structure in its place? Among all the men who supplied the materials and were responsible for the job not a single one had the capacity to take charge and act; they all allowed themselves to be more or less forced along and, under the force of clichés and the pressures of the moment, let themselves be lured into temporary expedients and half-baked schemes that could not last. Above all there was no organized and ably conducted information program; in its place arose a wild, uncouth, and pointless propaganda conducted by journalists who had meager knowledge, little sense of responsibility, and no political sense and banked solely on the masses' drive for power and survival. Those are the deeper causes of the great failure.

In the course of the Austrian revolution, particularly in Vienna, the miscellaneous character and immaturity of its intellectual assumptions became manifest. This is partly explained by the peculiar character of Austrian conditions, by the strong federalistic bent of the provinces, which never permitted the events in the capital to acquire the same towering and decisive importance as, say, developments in Paris had for France. Bound up with the separatist spirit of the provinces, which even Joseph II had been unable to overcome, were the various national interests, which were just beginning to develop and as yet possessed no fixed objectives. National interest drove the revolutionary movements apart in different directions: the Hungarians toward the emancipation of their own state, Lombardy to the idea of national unity under the leadership of Sardinia-Piedmont, the Czechs into the congress of Prague, and the Germans into the Frankfurt National Assembly. These elements, making for total dissolution and affecting the very existence of the state, were things the Reichsrat in Vienna had to take into account and come to terms with in upholding the idea of a common Austrian state. Also lacking were organized political parties, for which such imprecise concepts as "right," "left," and "center" provided only partial substitutes.

And finally the social question! Only a few—those who were slightly acquainted with French literature or, like Violand, knew about the doctrines of a Lorenz von Stein or the English labor movement —ventured into discussions of the principles involved, and then in a quite amateurish and superficial fashion. For the masses it was from the start a simple question of bread, and it became increasingly so when industry and commerce ground to a halt because of the events in Vienna and when dangerously mounting unemployment and hunger began to turn the revolution into anarchy. The suburban workers, leaderless, unorganized, and politically unschooled, at first acted only as the rugged *avant garde* of the liberal bourgeoisie. They demanded the ten-

hour day and increased wages but at the same time they wrecked the machines in the factories, depriving themselves of their jobs and proving how poorly they recognized their position in the modern economic system and how backward they really were. Thus the Viennese revolution was not accompanied by a corresponding intellectual development but was governed by the increasing deterioration of living conditions in the great city. The three phases of the revolution in Vienna—and they are limited to Vienna —the constitutional, the democratic, and the social revolutionary phases (or the March, May, and October revolutions), go hand in hand with growing impoverishment, drift, and intellectual confusion, with the gradual retreat of the disenchanted bourgeois intellectuals, and with mounting indifference on the part of the rural population, which had attained its primary objective with the abolition of patrimonial bonds of servitude, forced labor, and seignorial dues and now had to work out the problems stemming from this mighty advance. One should not forget how long a period of industrial development, political education, and intellectual progress in general was needed to give the workers the necessary inner strength and consciousness of their position in society; and that it was the liberal era that first prepared the way for and made possible the sociopolitical rise of the democratic elements. The attempt to bypass this time span, this phase of development, was bound to end in failure.

Suggested Additional Reading

The Austrian diplomat Count Hübner recorded in his diary that he had "noticed only one passion in Prince Metternich: writing. The amount of ink he has consumed in his life is almost beyond belief." The same is true of those who have written about Metternich; the literature on him is already vast and still growing. Fortunately, the student who wishes to pursue the subject beyond the samples in this volume can find expert guidance. Heinrich Ritter von Srbik, *Metternich, der Staatsmann und der Mensch* (2 vols.; Munich, 1925), besides being the preeminent biography, describes in its notes and introduction almost all the literature up to that time. The third volume, published posthumously (Munich, 1954), is essentially a critical bibliography of the works appearing in the intervening years. The most recent survey—and for English readers certainly the most convenient—is Paul W. Schroeder, "Metternich Studies since 1925," *Journal of Modern History,* XXXIII (1961), 237–260. Also of interest because of its emphasis on the great controversy initiated by Srbik is A. O. Meyer, "Der Streit um Metternich," *Historische Zeitschrift,* CLVII (1937), 75–84. For the most recent works, of course, one must thumb through the professional journals and other guides. The following suggestions include enough titles in English to keep the nonspecialist busy, but they also aim at providing the serious investigator with an up-to-date guide to the best available anywhere. The recommendations are selective and, with several exceptions, do not include the works already represented in this volume; reading the latter in their entirety would probably be the best way to begin.

Among the primary sources that have been printed, by all odds still the most important are the papers published by the Chancellor's son, Prince Richard Metternich, with the aid of Alfons von Klinkowström, under the title *Aus Metternich's nachgelassenen Papieren* (8 vols.; Vienna, 1880–1884). A comparison with the original family papers now housed in the *Státní Ústrední Archiv* in Prague indicates that the published version is surprisingly complete and accurate. It is not flawless, however, and the reader is particularly warned against the inaccuracies of the autobiographical fragment in the first volume. An English edition, entitled *Memoirs of Prince Metternich* (5 vols.; New York, 1880–1882) is incomplete, lacking most of all Metternich's later reflections and comments.

In addition to this basic collection there are many document publications devoted to specific topics. One popular work over the years is that edited by Jean Hanoteau, *Letters du Prince Metternich à la Comtesse de Lieven, 1818–19* (Paris, 1909). Although the Countess Lieven was his mistress, the letters have considerable philosophical and political value. By contrast it is mainly the love interest that parades through the correspondence recently edited by Maria Ullrichova, *Clemens Metternich—Wilhelmina von Sagan. Ein Briefwechsel, 1813–1815* (Graz and Cologne, 1966). It is instructive, however, to see the foreign minister in those hectic days mooning like a schoolboy. More important is Metternich's correspondence with Prince Wittgenstein published by Hans-Joachim Schoeps under the title "Metternichs Kampf gegen die Revolution. Weltanschauung in Briefen," *Historische Zeitschrift,* CCV (1967), 529–565. Another valuable collection is the private correspondence of Metternich and Richelieu published by Guillaume de Bertier de Sauvigny under the title, *France and the European Alliance, 1816-1821* (Notre Dame, Ind., 1958). For documents on many other specialized topics one should consult the above-mentioned guides as well as a recent article by A. C. Breycha-Vautier, "More Sources on Metternich," *Austrian History Yearbook,* I (1965), 38–44. For a representative sampling of the times, however, see the small collection edited by Mack Walker, *Metternich's Europe* (New York, 1968).

Biographies of Metternich are plentiful but, except for Srbik's monumental volumes, too short to cover the subject adequately. Arthur Herman, *Metternich* (London, 1932) is useful, but Srbik is probably right in claiming that it is essentially an unacknowledged abridgment of his own work (see his caustic review in the *Journal of Modern History,* V [1933], 100–102). Likewise influenced by Srbik but more extravagant in its priase of Metternich is Algernon Cecil, *Metternich, 1773-1859: A Study of His Period and Personality* (London, 1933). More original and with the stress on diplomacy is Helene du Coudray, *Metternich* (New Haven, Conn., 1936). As works of scholarship two books originally published in France are superior to the foregoing and make original contributions based on archival sources. These are Constantin de Grunwald, *Metternich* (English ed., London, 1953), and G. de Bertier de Sauvigny, *Metternich and His Times* (English ed., London, 1962). Bertier is now the world's leading Metternich scholar, and this book skillfully weaves together interesting excerpts from unpublished sources. The English edition contains a valuable chapter on the alliance system not present in the French original. Of similar quality but on a limited theme is the study of Conte Egon Cäsar Corti, *Metternich und die Frauen* (2 vols.; Zurich and Vienna, 1948-1949), which is a more serious work than the title suggests. His *Rise of the House of Rothschild* (New York and London, 1928) and his *Reign of the House of Rothschild* (New York, 1928) likewise throw light on Metternich's life. The most recent biography, Henry Valloton's *Metternich* (Paris: Fayard, 1965; German edition, Hamburg, 1966), collects in one place many judgments of Metternich but solves none of the problems and lacks scholarly apparatus.

Metternich's diplomacy has been the subject of many specialized monographs and general treatments. A lucid and well-informed introduction covering most of the period is Peter Richard Rohden, *Die klassische Diplomatie von Kaunitz bis Metternich* (Leipzig, 1939). Edward Vose Gulick, *Europe's Classical Balance of Power* (Ithaca, N. Y., 1955) ends with the Congress of Vienna as does the older but still important classic by Albert Sorel, *L'Europe et la révolution française* (8 vols.; Paris, 1885-1904). On Metternich's embassy to Paris 1806-1809, Josephine Branch Stearns, *The Role of Metternich in Undermining Napoleon* (Urbana, Ill., 1948) represents the view that Metternich wanted war; whereas Manfred Botzenhart, *Metternichs Pariser Botschafterzeit* (Münster, 1967), as previously mentioned in this volume, argues the opposite. On the period of Austrian subservience to Napoleon, Fedor von Demelitsch, *Metternich und seine auswärtige Politik* (Stuttgart, 1898) is still the standard work while C. S. B. Burkland, *Metternich and the British Government from 1809 to 1813* (London, 1932), is virtually definitive within its scope.

Metternich's policy during the War of Liberation has called forth many conflicting accounts. Alfred Greulich, *Österreichs Beitritt zur Koalition im Jahre 1813* (Leipzig, 1931) uses archival sources and intricate reasoning to show that Metternich wanted no break with Napoleon in 1813. Emil Lauber, *Metternichs Kampf um die europäische Mitte* (Vienna and Leipzig, 1939) rejects this view and attempts to make Metternich a champion of Pan-Germanism in his struggle for *Mitteleuropa.* Hellmuth Rössler (whose biography of Stadion is discussed elsewhere in this volume) first developed his ideas in *Österreichs Kampf um Deutschlands Befreiung* (2 vols.; Hamburg, 1940), blaming Metternich precisely because he disdained German nationalism. On the Congress of Vienna the older work by C. K. Webster, *The Congress of Vienna, 1814-15* (London, 1919) retains its traditional value, but the best study now is Karl Griewank, *Der Wiener Kongress und die Neuordnung*

Europas 1814/15 (Leipzig, 1942), while an article by Srbik, "Metternichs Plan einer Neuordnung Europas 1814/15," *Mitteilungen des österreichischen Instituts für Geschichtsforschung,* XL (1925), 109–126, is indispensable. Metternich's role at the Congress of Vienna is also dealt with in works covering more ground. Among these are Henry A. Kissinger, *A World Restored,* discussed elsewhere in this book; Harold G. Nicolson, *The Congress of Vienna: A Study in Allied Unity, 1812–1822* (New York, 1946); C. K. Webster's classic work, *The Foreign Policy of Castlereagh, 1812–1822* (2 vols.; vol. I: London, 1931; vol. II: London, 1925); and the excellent W. Alison Phillips, *The Confederation of Europe, A Study of the European Alliance, 1813–1823, as an Experiment in the International Organization of Peace* (London, 1913).

The last-named study was ahead of its time, the first of a number of works dealing explicitly with the alliance system as something more than conventional diplomacy. Among the more important of these are Werner Näf's "Versuche gesamteuropäischer Organisation und Politik in den ersten Jahrzehnten des 19. Jahrhunderts" in his *Staat und Staatsgedanke. Vorträge zur neueren Geschichte* (Bonn, 1935); the same author's *Zur Geschichte der heiligen Allianz* (Bern, 1928); and the works of his students: Hans W. Schmalz, *Versuche einer gesamteuropäischen Organisation, 1815–1820* (Aarau, Switz., 1940) and Hans Reiben, *Prinzipiengrundlage und Diplomatie in Metternichs Europapolitik, 1815–1848* (Aarau, 1942). Of the books dealing specifically with the Holy alliance, the best is probably Maurice Bourquin, *Histoire de la Sainte-Alliance* (Geneva, 1954), and Metternich's diplomacy as a whole is nowhere more sagely assessed than in the essay by Robert A. Kann, "Metternich: A Reappraisal of His Impact on International Relations," *Journal of Modern History,* XXXII (1960), 333–339. Metternich also figures prominently in an article by Enno E. Kraehe, "Foreign Policy and the Nationality Problem in the Habsburg Monarchy, 1800–1867," *Austrian History Yearbook,* vol. III, Pt. 3 (1967), pp. 3–36.

A number of works treat Metternich's re-lations with particular countries. G. de Bertier de Sauvigny, *Metternich et la France après le congrès de Vienne* (2 vols; Paris, 1968–1970) so far extends to 1824 and when complete will be the definitive work. Viktor Bibl, *Metternich in neuer Beleuchtung* (Vienna, 1928) deals with Germany in the early 1830s. George T. Romani, *The Neapolitan Revolution, 1820–1821* (Evanston, Ill., 1950); G. F. H. and J. Berkeley, *Italy in the Making, 1815–1848* (3 vols.; London, 1932–1940); and A. J. P. Taylor, *The Italian Problem in European Diplomacy* (Manchester, Eng., 1934) treat Italian affairs, but the reader should also consult the aforementioned guides for the excellent studies available in Italian. For England, H. W. V. Temperley, *The Foreign Policy of Canning* (London, 1925) and C. K. Webster, *The Foreign Policy of Palmerston, 1830–1841* (2 vols.; London, 1951) are standard works. Regrettably there is no comprehensive work specifically devoted to Metternich's Russian policy, but much material can be found in histories of the Near Eastern question and the alliance system.

Various interpretations of Metternich's principles can be found in E. L. Woodward, *Three Studies in European Conservatism* (London, 1929); Peter Viereck, *Conservatism Revisited; The Revolt against Revolt, 1815–1849* (New York and London, 1949); and E. Kittel, "Metternichs politische Grundanschauungen," *Historische Vierteljahrschrift,* XXIV (1929), 443–483. Kittel explicitly criticizes Srbik's views as set forth in the fourth selection in this volume. On Austrian internal affairs Anton Springer, *Geschichte Österreichs seit dem Wiener Frieden, 1809* (2 vols.; Leipzig, 1863) is still useful despite its outmoded criticism of Metternich. The best general history of Austria is that by Hugo Hantsch, *Die Geschichte Österreichs* (2 vols.; Vienna-Graz, 1937 and 1950), previously quoted in this volume, but see also C. A. Macartney, *The Habsburg Empire, 1790–1918* (London, 1968). More nearly centered on Metternich are Donald E. Emerson, *Metternich and the Political Police: Security and Subversion in the Hapsburg Monarchy* (The Hague, 1968); R. W. Seton-Watson, "Metternich and Internal Austrian

Policy," *Slavonic Review,* XVII (1939), 539–555, and XVIII (1939), 129–141; and Josef Karl Mayr, *Geschichte der österreichischen Staatskanzlei im Zeitalter des Fürsten Metternichs* (Vienna, 1935). R. John Rath, *The Provisional Austrian Regime in Lombardy-Venetia, 1814–1815* (Austin, Tex., 1969) is a definitive treatment of that subject.

Much valuable material on Metternich is also available in works on his associates. Among the best are Paul R. Sweet, *Friedrich von Gentz, Defender of the Old Order* (Madison, Wis., 1941); Alfred Ritter von Arneth, *Johann Freiherr von Wessenberg* (2 vols.; Vienna and Leipzig, 1898); and Emmanuel de Lévis-Mirepoix, *Un Collaborateur de Metternich; Mémoires et papiers de Lebzeltern* (Paris, 1949). As to the revolutions of 1848, R. John Rath, *The Viennese Revolution of 1848* (Austin, Tex., 1957) and William L. Langer, *Political and Social Upheaval, 1832–1852* (New York, Evanston, Ill., and London, 1969), though not focused on Metternich, are highly recommended, the latter for its bibliography as well.

Finally, of the many general works vital to Metternich studies, it is possible to list only a few. Heinrich von Srbik, *Deutsche Einheit: Die Idee und Wirklichkeit vom Heiligen Reich bis Königgrätz* (4 vols.; Munich, 1935–1942) elaborates the master's *grossdeutsche* philosophy, while Erich Marcks, *Der Aufsteig des Reiches. Deutsche Geschichte von 1807–1871/78* (2 vols.; Stuttgart and Berlin, 1936), offers a pro-Prussian rebuttal. Franz Schnabel, *Deutsche Geschichte im neunzehnten Jahrhundert* (4 vols.; 2d. ed., Freiburg, 1949) is more comprehensive and more detached than the other two. For Europe as a whole A. J. May, *The Age of Metternich, 1814–1848* (New York, 1933) is still the most convenient survey and certainly preferable to a work from East Germany: Werner Mayer, *Vormärz: die Ära Metternichs* (Potsdam, 1948). The latter is a Marxist view but differs little from the nineteenth-century liberal indictment of Metternich. Though subject to similar criticism to some extent, a more sophisticated East German work, based on original research, is Karl Obermann, *Deutschland von 1815 bis 1849* (3d ed. Berlin: 1967). From any point of view, however, there is still much that needs to be done on Prince Metternich.